Louis Trégance, Henry Crocker

Adventures in New Guinea

Nine Years in Captivity among the Orangwoks

Louis Trégance, Henry Crocker

Adventures in New Guinea
Nine Years in Captivity among the Orangwoks

ISBN/EAN: 9783337339593

Printed in Europe, USA, Canada, Australia, Japan

Cover: Foto ©ninafisch / pixelio.de

More available books at **www.hansebooks.com**

ADVENTURES IN NEW GUINEA

THE NARRATIVE OF LOUIS TRÉGANCE

A French Sailor

NINE YEARS IN CAPTIVITY AMONG THE ORANGWOKS
A TRIBE IN THE INTERIOR OF NEW GUINEA

EDITED, AND WITH AN INTRODUCTION, BY
THE REV. HENRY CROCKER
INCUMBENT OF ST. ANNE'S, WEBUMAI, N.Z.

NEW AND CHEAPER EDITION

LONDON
SAMPSON LOW, MARSTON & COMPANY
Limited
St. Dunstan's House
FETTER LANE, FLEET STREET, E.C.
1894

[*All rights reserved*]

LONDON:
PRINTED BY GILBERT AND RIVINGTON, LD.,
ST. JOHN'S HOUSE, CLERKENWELL ROAD, E.C.

INTRODUCTION.

The following narrative contains the life and adventures of Louis Trégance, while in captivity among the Orangwöks, a tribe inhabiting the interior of New Guinea, from which place he made his escape to the continent of Australia. However, it will be better that he should tell his own story, contained in the following narrative; and in introducing it to the public, I will simply explain how I came to accept the task of preparing it for the press, and to what extent I am responsible for what is here written. In the beginning of March (the 7th of that month, I find from my note-book), I was called in to visit a sick parishioner—a young man, a stranger to the place. He was suffering from an attack of typhoid fever, and was exceedingly ill. He was apparently about thirty-five years old, and his face was well bronzed. He was the mate of a colonial vessel, and had been taken ill on her arrival in port. His friend the captain, Philip Rigaud, had left him under the care of the people of the house, and had otherwise provided for his necessities. On his recovery he was to join his ship at Newcastle, whither she had sailed about a week before. All this I learned from the people in whose care he was left. I saw him constantly after this, until he recovered, and was able to get about. Finding him an intelligent man, and knowing him to be without friends in the place, I invited him frequently to come and spend an hour or so with me, during his period of convalescence. As he accepted my invitation we had many opportunities of conversing together, and on one of these occasions he told me something of his history. I immediately saw, as I thought, the importance of his story, and pressed him to put his adventures upon paper. This he ultimately did, and the following pages are the result.

My part as editor is soon explained. I have assisted to express the author's meaning more clearly, by making occasional alterations in the words used, and in the construction of his sentences. Generally, however, I found his style clear, and perfectly intelligible, so that my labour in this respect was very slight.

A few notes have also been appended,

where they have seemed to me to be required.
As the author had several sketches of the
scenery of New Guinea in his possession, I
obtained his permission to have these copied.
They are published with the narrative, and
will help to elucidate the narrative itself.
In reference to these sketches I must explain,
first, that the originals were roughly done;
they were evidently the work of a self-taught
man; and that they were more or less
defaced, as they had been in his possession
for a long time; and, lastly, that I obtained
the assistance of my friend Mr. Hull in preparing them for publication, and his artistic
skill has been brought to bear upon them.
Trégance has also in his possession a sketch
of Lamlam. And although he was unwilling
that this should be copied, yet he has allowed
me to describe the face and expression which
were represented in that portrait. An oval
face, olive-coloured—with large, lustrous,
sad-looking eyes—nose of the Grecian type
—hair straight and black, but not long.
Such were the principal features of the
portrait of Lamlam. The expression was
pleasing, but melancholy. These remarks
will not, I hope, be without interest to those
who read the chapters referring to the person
who is thus described.

As the true character of the book is evident to the careful reader, it is unnecessary that more should be said by way of introduction to it.

HENRY CROCKER.

ST. ANN'S PARSONAGE,
 WĔRĔMAI N.Z.

PREFACE.

The clergyman who has been kind enough to revise this narrative of my adventures in New Guinea, has explained how it came to be given to the world. I have, therefore, only to say, that what I have selected from my notes and recollections of the kingdom of K'ootar is but a small portion of the whole; yet it contains, probably, the most striking and interesting facts which came under my knowledge. There are some subjects on which I am not able to speak with that information which could make my words of real value—as, for instance, the nature of the trees and flowers of the country—the various kinds of animals which are found in New Guinea—at best I can only describe, and that very imperfectly, such things as came under my own observation. Of those things, therefore, I have said but little. Of the habits, customs, and beliefs of the people, I can speak more fully, as it did not require more than the possession of average intelligence to enable me to understand what I saw and heard during my nine years' residence among the Orangwöks. Any further information that lies in my power to give will be given with pleasure to those who seek it.

Louis Trégance.

Ship "Newcastle,"
September, 1875.

LIST OF ILLUSTRATIONS.

	PAGE
Punishment of Criminals . . .	*Frontispiece*
The Wild Sea	*To face* 44
The Capture	,, 66
Map of New Guinea . . .	,, 128
The Trial	,, 219

ADVENTURES IN NEW GUINEA.

CHAPTER I.

I was born in the Province of Maine, in a little village on its southern border, and until I was nearly twelve years old I knew very little of the world outside my native village. Before I was seven years old my father taught me to read, and this was all the schooling I got until I left home, for my father died when I reached the age of seven. He was a good man, I am sure, for I can remember many of the lessons he gave me about God and Christ, and how he taught me always to do what I knew to be right, without fearing man.

He did not fear the curé as much as my mother did; indeed he did not fear him at all, for he always spoke his opinions freely in the curé's presence, and was not afraid to argue with him. My mother, on the contrary, was always afraid of the priest, and would scold my father, when they were alone, for not showing greater reverence to the priest of God. At this my father would laugh, and reply, "Do you think, wife, that the great and good God would give to such men as our priests the power to bless or curse His creatures? Depend upon it, God loves His creatures too well to leave them in the hands of any deputy. The Emperor appoints officers to take the oversight of his empire, because he cannot overlook everything himself; and see what mismanagement arises through the negligence of his officers. But God, who is everywhere, requires no deputies to act for Him. The curé is a good man, and as such I respect him, yet he has no power either to bless or curse God's people."

This was a long speech for my father to make, but I remember it, for he often said the same thing to me while he was teaching me.

It was a great loss as well as a great sorrow to me when my dear father died.

We had always been poor, even when he lived, and after his death we were poorer than ever; so now I got no more teaching, for I was required to spend all my time in assisting my mother in various ways.

I learnt the Paternoster and the Credo from the curé, and this was all I knew of religion, except what my father had taught me.

During all the week I was kept at work, and had little time for play; but when Sunday came, after prayers and sermon from the curé, we all assembled in the open park for our games, and then I played until I was tired out, after which I slept soundly till Monday came again.

Although there were many hardships in that early part of my life, for food was scarce at times, and the winters were trying with such poor clothes as we wore, yet I was happy, and I look back to those early years with feelings of regret.

When I was about ten years old, I remember going to another village with Philip Rigaud, who was two years older than myself. My mother had given me a holiday, for she was also dressed for one, although she did not come with us.

She told me to take a long day, and gave me plenty of food to take with me. So Philip and I sauntered along the high road very happy, for we were fast friends. Philip told me stories about the sea, and I asked him what the sea was like.

"Dost thou not know, Louis?" (My name is Louis Trégance.)

"No, how can I, Philip? I have never been away from our little village."

"But did not thy father teach thee?"

Then seeing that he had awakened in me a painful memory, he said,—

"Come, Louis, I will take thee to a place where thou shalt see the great ocean, and I will tell thee all that I know about it. And then we will go to Blanc, the old gardener, who has travelled on the sea, and he will tell us stories about his adventures when he was a sailor."

About seven miles from our village there was a high hill, so high that none of us children ever cared to climb it, and from the top of this hill Philip said the ocean could be seen. So, excited by the words of Philip, I consented to join him in climbing to its top, that we might catch a glimpse of the new world where men lived in houses that moved along driven by the wind, without breaking up, and that carried them to new places every day, so that they never saw the same place two days together. After several hours' hard walking, broken by intervals of resting, we reached a high peak of the hill. So eager was I to see this new world of which Philip had told me, that I rushed up the last slope of the ascent, breathless though I was from our long journey, and looked eagerly around. I could see nothing but hills, plains, and houses, (I had never imagined them to be so numerous,) and a dull, leaden-looking cloud beyond them all.

"Alas! Philip," I cried to him, "it is not here—the ocean of which you spoke."

"See, my friend," he replied, pointing to the dull leaden clouds, "see, that is the ocean, look," and, following the direction of his hand, I gazed intently, and saw a speck of white moving. "Is that a bird?" I asked.

"No, that is a ship; she is moving across the water that you see so far away." And now I could perceive that that which I had mistaken for a cloud was unlike one—that it was a broad plain, and that a ship was moving across it. As I looked, the sun, which had been hidden since we had been standing here, came out, and then a sheet of light illuminated the ship's pathway, which became like burnished gold.

"See, Philip, how beautiful!" I exclaimed, in an ecstasy of delight. My companion was charmed with my enthusiasm, for the sight was commonplace to him. He had lived near the sea before coming to our village.

This day was an eventful one to me; for on my return home, very late and very tired, I found M. Cobót, one of the villagers that I had never liked, at home with my mother.

He had often been to our house lately, and I had not liked him any the more on that account. To-night he was sitting before the fire when I entered the room, and my mother was standing by his side, his arm was round her waist, and she appeared as if she had just risen from his knee. She at once came to me, and, kissing me, said, "Come, mon fils, let me present thee to thy new father, M. Cobót." I could not believe I had heard aright; I was filled with indignation, and, regardless of consequences, replied, "He is not my father; my father is in the grave, and I wish I was with him." On hearing this speech, which was a very rude one (and I can only excuse it by saying I was very tired), my poor mother burst into tears, and my step-father (for he was married to my mother), rising from his seat, spoke severely to me, threatening me for my conduct to my mother. This recalled me to myself, and, after kissing my mother and apologizing to my step-father, I shrank away to my room. Of course this was a bad beginning, and did not incline M. Cobót to look upon me with favour.

Next morning, before anybody was stirring, I got up and walked to the cemetery. I had been accustomed to go there with my mother in the happy days that were gone, to look at the neat little grave of my father, to arrange the wooden cross at its head, and to lay a few flowers on the green turf. When I reached there my heart was full of sorrow, and, throwing myself on the cold grave, I spoke to my father and told him all the trouble that was in his child's heart. In a little while I felt calmer, and was able to return home in a more contented mood. Yet I resolved I would never call M. Cobót father. The day passed off well enough, for my stepfather never took any notice of me after the first morning salutation. Had he always acted in this way all would have been well, and I should have spent all my days in France, instead of wandering in strange lands; but he conceived as violent a dislike to me as I had taken to him, and treated me very cruelly at times in spite of my mother's entreaties on my behalf. Two years were spent in this way, and in secret intercourse with Philip and Blanc the gardener, who fired our boyish imaginations with stories of the sea and foreign countries where he had travelled. Philip and I had a thought in our hearts which gradually grew into action. We talked it over between ourselves until we came to think it entirely practicable. We resolved to leave the village, to travel to a sea-port, and become sailors. This idea expanded itself in our imaginations until we could no longer free ourselves from its fascination. After a fresh instance of M. Cobót's cruelty I arranged with Philip that we would leave on a certain morning very early. This was in the autumn, and then I went home to make preparations for running away. Ah, how sorry I felt when I saw my poor mother's pale face and knew I should leave her behind me! I wound my arms round her and kissed her. This unwonted instance of affection surprised her, but she took me into her arms, and, sitting down, talked to me.

"Louis, I wish thou wouldst try to love M. Cobót for my sake. He will then be kind to thee, poor child!"

My tears fell fast as I sobbed out my reply. "I will always think of him kindly for your sake, ma mère; but I cannot give him the love which belongs to my own father."

She sighed as I kissed her again and asked her forgiveness for all my acts of naughtiness. During the evening M. Cobót was kinder to me than usual, and my mother took many opportunities of expressing her love for me. Such kindness well-nigh took away all my resolve to leave home. Yet I made my

preparations, which were soon made, and got
to my room at an earlier hour than usual,
after kissing my mother with great affection.
My excitement kept me awake for a long
time, so that I heard my mother preparing
for her bed. She came to me before she went,
and, turning down the bed-clothes, as she was
wont to do, looked at me and kissed me again.
I threw my arms round her and returned her
embrace. "Good night, Louis, the good
God keep thee!" and so she left me. Again
my resolution faltered, and I had nearly given
up all idea of running off, when a gentle tap
came at my window. This was the signal
agreed upon between Philip and myself. At
once I sprang up, and, dressing myself
quietly, was soon in the presence of my comrade. "Courage, mon ami," said Philip.
"Soon we shall be on the great ocean and
shall return laden with wealth. Courage!"
And indeed I needed some strengthening at
this moment, for the memory of all my
mother's love and of M. Cobót's new kindness
was upon me. We had decided to keep the
high road until daylight, when we were to
turn off into the by-ways and strike across
the country. We hoped in this way to avoid
any hue and cry that might be raised, and so
pursue our course to the sea unmolested.

We walked steadily along the main road for about four hours, and made good progress. At sunrise we halted and made a hearty breakfast out of our small stock of food. As the sun was well up in the heavens before we had rested ourselves sufficiently, on resuming our journey we decided to turn off the main road at once. This we did, taking our route across fields and meadows. If there was any pursuit of us, we thus avoided our pursuers.

It is not necessary that I should relate all the incidents of those wearisome days. Suffice it to say that we often wished ourselves home again, for we were frequently hungry and weary, and always in fear, either of falling into the hands of the officer of police, or of those of our pursuers, and so being carried back ignominiously to our homes. As we were frequently without food, for our little stock lasted us barely two days, and we had to depend upon the charity of the people of the country through which we were passing, and always had to lie out at night, our hardships began to tell upon us, and we became gaunt and emaciated in appearance Still we kept up under the hope that some day we should be at our destination—the nearest sea-port—and then should realize our long-cherished hope. So we toiled on until, on the tenth day, when all heart was passing from us, Philip suddenly exclaimed, "See, Louis, there is the ocean!" And, indeed, there it was straight before us. We had just turned the point of a hill which ran into the road. There lay the ocean, quite close, not more than two or three miles from us. I could see the huge waves, wrapped in their white foam, rolling upon the shore. And now I could understand the noise which had been filling my ears for a long time. It was the roll of the surf upon the beach, and soon we saw the masts of ships, like a forest, and as I carried my eye along, houses, churches, and public buildings, such as I had never seen before, came into view.

"This is our destination," said Philip. "Let us hasten." In about an hour we entered the town. The streets were filled with people, but nobody took any notice of us. We were ashamed of our poor clothing and miserable appearance. But we attracted no notice from the lazy people who thronged the streets. We pressed on, feeling very hungry and sick, for we had been more than twenty-four hours without food.

"Philip," I said, "I must have something to eat; I am sick."

"Stay, mon ami, I will get you food;

courage, my little companion;" and, leaving me near a baker's shop, Philip darted off, and began to address himself to the passers-by. At times he pointed to me, and one of the persons addressed by him, putting his hand in his pocket, gave him something. My comrade rushed back to me, and, holding up a franc piece, said,—

"Courage, Louis, we shall have food."

After satisfying our hunger, we again pushed on until we reached the harbour. At last we stood upon the wharf and looked upon the vast ships, whose sides rose many feet above the level of the planks on which we stood. In order to reach their decks we should have had to climb up a ladder, and we had not the courage to do this; so we continued walking along until we came to a vessel whose deck was flush with the wharf. Philip immediately went on board, and after some hesitation I followed him. The man to whom Philip spoke, asking him to take us as cabin-boys, replied, after looking closely at each of us in turn,—

"So, my little men, you want to be sailors, to leave Belle France, to tread over the wide world? Well, as I happen to want two little men, and you are likely boys, I will take you in my ship, the *Ville du Havre*. So come aboard and enter your names on the ship's books," he said, with a smile.

Surprised and overjoyed at this unexpected answer to our first application, we hurried to obey the direction of the man, who turned out to be the first mate. After some inquiry as to our names, ages, and place of residence, we were sent below to dinner, which was, we thought, like the dinner of a king.

The result of our application was that we were accepted as apprentices (although not registered) on board of the *Ville du Havre*, sailing next day for Liverpool. Philip and I fell into our bunks that night with feelings of the deepest satisfaction and thankfulness.

CHAPTER II.

The *Ville du Havre*, of which the captain and the mate were part-owners, drew out into the Channel early in the morning, and made ready to sail. For some reason Philip and I were kept below until we were well out of the harbour, when we were allowed to go on deck and expected to make ourselves useful. As soon as we met the fresh breeze the ship began to dance and roll, creating strange sensations in us. This was the terrible mal de mer, of which one never hears enough, and never thinks enough, until one has experienced it oneself. I cannot say how I felt, except that I felt sick, and yet I was not sick. My head began to ache, my brain began to reel as if I would fall, and I did not care to stand upright.

"Oh, Philip!" I said, "this is dreadful! What is the matter with us?" For he was as pale as one dead.

"This is sea-sickness, Louis. It will soon be over. Keep a brave heart, my friend."

The kind mate came to us, and told us to

lie down for a little while, which we gladly did. As the wind increased the ship rose and fell as if she was jumping over the waves, and then I felt as if the whole of my inside was coming into my mouth. I tried to cry out to Philip, but I vomited the instant I opened my mouth. I continued this vomiting for several minutes, which continued until my mouth filled with some bitter stuff, and after this I felt easier, and lay down. I continued ill for several days, for we had a head wind, and during all this time I wished myself back again with my dear mother and M. Cobót. I often saw the village, with its little church and the kind curé; the quiet cemetery, where lay my father; the park, in which the boys and girls assembled to dance; and then my mind wandered back to the fields of rich corn, the thick clustering grapes. I would have given anything for a taste of the ripe grapes at this moment; and then I felt how foolish I had been to leave the beautiful and quiet earth, to trust myself to the heaving, unstable sea! I resolved, if ever I got back again to France, to content myself with such happiness as she could afford me.

But trouble cannot last for ever, and so my sickness and nausea came to an end before we reached Liverpool, which we were seven days in doing. And when I got about on the deck, climbing the masts, and helping to pull the ropes, I began again to like the idea of being a sailor. Still I was glad when Liverpool was reached, and when we drew up by the side of the long wharf to change our cargo I worked hard to help, for I felt I ought to do all I could for the kind friend who had taken me on board.

Philip worked better than I did, and was more useful. He was stronger, and began to look fat and be amusing to the men, with whom he was a great favourite. He was, however, always my friend, and ready to help me or to defend me.

Sometimes he and I were allowed to walk in the strange English city, among the crowds of people, and we were much astonished by all that we saw. One day we walked a long way, until we came to the country, where there were many trees, and crowds of people dressed so well, and rich carriages, and beautiful horses, and there was gay music playing. The men and women, or ladies and gentlemen, as Philip called them, were so happy as they laughed and talked. One young lady looked at us, and I saw a look of pity pass into her face. She touched the arm of the old gentleman who was seated near her, and he too glanced at us. I felt ashamed that we were so poor, for our clothes did not fit us ; they had been given to us by the sailors, and had been cut down to our size. The young lady was like an angel, so sweet was her smile of pity. I could have gazed for ever on her face, but Philip drew me away, and soon we began to return on our route to the ship, I feeling very sad to think that I was shut out from all this world that I saw now for the first time.

We could not understand the people, but sometimes they spoke to us and pointed after us—the baser sort, I mean, the gamins of that great city. Still we took no notice, for we did not understand the words they used, although we knew they were not complimentary to Philip and myself.

I did not get strong, even after the lapse of some weeks, and often had a violent pain in my head. This was a new experience for me, for I had always been a healthy boy when at home. This pain continued for some days, which caused me great sorrow, as I felt I was not doing enough work for our kind friend the mate. The ship was nearly full, and was getting ready to sail, this time for America.

One day I had felt worse than ever, and was very weak. Philip and I walked in the street not far from the ship, for I could not walk very far, and as we walked I felt a strange sensation come over me, and then I fell to the ground. When I came to myself I was in a large room, very clean and nice-looking, and was lying on a little bed. The large room was full of similar beds, on which were lying sick people. This was a hospital. I did not know this at once, for I could not understand what the nurse said to me; and Philip was not with me. Soon a gentleman, well-dressed and quick in his manner, entered the room. This was the doctor. He came at once to my bed. After speaking to the nurse he turned to me and said in my own language,—

"Well, my little man, what is the matter with you?"

I replied by telling him what befell me in the street.

After examining my pulse and tongue, he said,—

"You will not be able to go in your ship this voyage, my boy; you have a touch of fever upon you, and you must stay where you are for some weeks at least."

Soon after this I slept, and when I awoke

Philip and the mate were by my side. They had seen the doctor, who had told them about my fever, so they said,—"We shan't see you for a long time, Louis, as we are going to sail in two days to America. But keep a look out for the *Ville du Havre* on her return, and we will then take you with us." So we shook hands, Philip kissing me as they went away. I was sorry, yet I was too ill to think much just now.

Many days passed—some weeks, I think—before I began to get better, and during all the time I was carefully tended by the doctor and the nurse. When I was getting better there came one day into the room a young lady. She came to visit the sick and to read to them. I thought her face was not strange to me, and when she came to my bed and smiled on me I recognized her again. It was the young lady I had seen in the cemetery. She spoke to me in English, and on my replying in French that I did not understand, she immediately answered me in my own tongue.

"You have been very ill, my poor boy!" she said, laying her hand on my hot head.

"Yes, mademoiselle," I replied; "of fever, but I am better now, thank the saints."

She looked at me when I said this, very earnestly and pityingly, and said, "I am glad you are thankful that God is making you well. It is He who has been so good to you. Try and thank Him in your heart. Would you like me to read to you something about Him?"

"Yes, yes, mademoiselle; my father used to tell me about Him before he died. But I have not heard about the good God since that sad event."

Without saying more the young lady opened a little book which she carried in her hand and read. It told about Jesus receiving sinners and eating with them, and then about a man losing one sheep in the wilderness, next of the woman who lost a piece of money, and last of the two sons, one of whom went into a far country. This, I thought, was like myself running away from my mother; and when she read of the good father seeing his son while he was yet a long way off, and being glad at his coming back, I thought of my kind mother watching for me—ready to welcome me home again, and I wept. The kind lady, who had explained all this story to me in French, asked me about my mother, and I told her all my story. After asking me where my mother lived, she took her leave, promising to come and see me again.

Three days after the young lady came again, bringing me a beautiful book with pictures in it. The book was in French— the "Pilgrim's Progress"—but, alas! I could not read it, I could only read the little words, so she read some of the story to me, and left the book for me that I might look at the pictures.

Through all the kindness I received I soon got well, and was able to sit up, and then to get out into the air. The doctor told me I should be able to leave the hospital in a week or two, but that I could not do any heavy work, as I was not strong. On my telling this to the kind lady, she asked me where I thought of going. I said I did not know, but I would inquire so soon as I had left the good hospital. Next time she came the old gentleman her father was with her, and, after questioning me, he said, "As you are ready to leave the hospital, Louis, I will take you into my service until you are strong, so you can come with me to-day, if you like."

I jumped at this kind offer, and expressed my readiness to go with him and the young lady at once. So I was soon, after thanking the good doctor and the nurse for their kindness to me, on the box-seat of the gentleman's carriage. As the gentleman had provided me with a suit of clothes, clean and well-fitting, I did not feel ashamed of my dress, yet I felt ashamed to sit beside the man who drove the carriage. He was so fine, yet he was good to me, although I did not understand his words.

After I had been at Mr. Cunningham's for a few weeks, a letter came from my mother in reply to one which Miss Cunningham had written to her. My mother was glad to learn that I had fallen among kind friends, and begged me to communicate with her.

With the assistance of my mistress, I sent a letter to my mother, asking her pardon and blessing. After the lapse of many weeks another letter came, conveying the forgiveness which I sought, and giving me permission to remain where I was.

I was very happy in the service of Mr. Cunningham, and remained with him four years. During this time I made progress in reading and writing the English language, as well as in speaking it. His daughter, my first kind friend, allowed me to be taken to the English church, where I was charmed by the fact that I could understand every word of the prayers, and could hear the words of the holy God in English (for I had now learned to speak English). I became a Protestant, a step which I have never since regretted, for I have thus been taught to depend more upon my conscience than upon the minister for guidance, and this self-direction promotes a sense of responsibility which induces one to read and think for oneself. The habit of doing so has been most valuable to me in my wandering life, and although I have doubtless fallen into many errors, yet I have also been saved from perpetrating many serious offences which I should have committed had I not learned to interrogate my conscience in respect of all my duties.

Four years passed away, and I never saw anything of Philip. For once, when the *Ville du Havre* came to Liverpool, I was away in the country, whither the family had gone for a change. Great was my disappointment when I heard that the ship had been in, and that Philip had been to Mr. Cunningham's house inquiring for me. He left word that the *Ville du Havre* was going to Australia, and might not be back in port for two years. In spite of my great disappointment in missing my old friend, I was very happy in my present service, and should have remained there had it not been for a great calamity which befell my master. Miss Harriette, for that was the young lady's name, was always delicate, and this rendered her susceptible of any sickness that was infectious. After I had been the time I have mentioned in her father's service, she caught an infectious disease, and, in spite of all the efforts of the many skilful medical men who were called in to attend on her, she died. I felt the blow very greatly, the more so as she was not conscious when she died, and had not been so for several days before the sad event, and could not therefore bid us good-bye. Ah! dearest and best of my earliest friends, I have never ceased to think of thee and to lament thy early death! For although thou wert exalted far beyond my lowly station, yet thy sympathy, which was as an angel's, bridged over that gulf which had been otherwise impassable.

Farewell! thou art now in the bosom of the Jesus thou didst love, and of whom thou didst speak to thy fallen brother. Farewell, dear Miss Harriette!

The death of Miss Harriette led to many changes, for she was an only child, and although I could have remained in the service of Mr. Cunningham, yet I was now anxious to get away from the scenes which continually reminded me of my late beloved mistress. Again the old longing for a sea life awoke in me, and I read eagerly every book I came across which related to sea-life, and had my imagination fired with the idea of foreign travels. I thought constantly of Philip, and wondered if I should ever meet him again, picturing his surprise and delight if I should meet him in some distant part of the world.

With such thoughts I often walked upon the wharf and took a deep interest in the shipping. One afternoon, as I was thus employed, I came to a ship which was just being berthed, and I stood by to watch the warping operation. Her stern, with name clear and distinct, came round just where I stood, and I read with surprise and delight the words *Ville du Havre*. Immediately I went on board, and, walking straight to a fine young man who stood upon the poop, directing the operation, said, "Philip, my friend."

The young man stared for a moment, and then said, "You are mistaken, sir; my name is Philip, but you are a stranger to me."

"Philip, mon ami, dost thou not remember Louis?" I exclaimed, speaking to him in French.

Looking eagerly at me again, he immediately replied, embracing me,—

" Yes, yes, mon bon Louis; but how much thou art altered! Thou art a gentleman, and see," he said proudly, " I am the second mate of the *Ville du Havre.* Come to my cabin, Louis."

Need I say that, with my present feelings, sad at the loss of my late dear mistress, and full of cravings for adventures, I shipped on board Philip's vessel when she was ready to sail, confident, though I was only a sailor before the mast, yet that Philip would treat me as his old friend, and smooth away, as far as possible, the difference that lay between an officer and a common sailor? The ship was bound to Australia, where she had been for the last three years, for she was now the property of her captain and first mate, who were their own agents and directors.

CHAPTER III.

As I could write a good hand I was occasionally required to make entries in the log-book. This gave me a taste for the kind of entries which appear in such nautical diaries, so I started one on my own account, and have since, with more or less of intermission, kept up the practice of writing down the principal incidents of my life. A few extracts from my own log-book will show the reader the character of our outward voyage.

"*Oct.* 19.—Left the Bay of Biscay, after tumbling about in it for seven days, during the whole of which I was very sick, often wishing myself back with good Mr. Cunningham. Could not imagine what tempted me to leave the comfort of shore-life for the sea. Now, however, that I am getting well, and that we have a bright sun and a clear sky, with a fresh wind abaft, I begin to enjoy the sea. The motion is pleasant, and it amuses me to watch the sea-birds sailing along to outstrip the *Ville du Havre.*"

"*Oct.* 22.—Still a fair wind. The man at the mast-head sung out early this morning, 'Sail ho,' and, looking to leeward, saw the white sail of a vessel crossing our course. Made her out a barque-rigged ship. In a couple of hours, as she was directly on our course, we hailed her. She proved to be the *New Jersey*, bound for London."

"*Nov.* 3.—We are now in the tropics, and the weather is insufferable during the day, although it is sometimes pleasanter at night. We lay becalmed for several days, and as there was a large ship in the same condition a few miles off, we obtained the captain's permission to visit her. She was the *Clyde*, from Melbourne, homeward bound, with a cargo of wool and gold. Hearing that she was a gold ship, I made inquiries as to where and how the gold was obtained, and learned that there were 'diggings' in Australia, where men congregated in large numbers to gather the precious metal. In the afternoon several of the men had a bathe, one of them swimming a long way from the ship. Shortly after his return to the vessel a large shark was seen to swim round her—a narrow escape for the Swede."

"*Nov.* 30.—Nearing the Cape; weather terribly cold, and coming in icy, cutting squalls from the south. Ship pitching and tossing very much—feel sick again."

"*Dec.* 2.—Yesterday we saw several tall peaks, which Philip told me were icebergs. They glittered when the rays of the sun fell on them once or twice. Cold still continues, and the waves very heavy."

"*Dec.* 3.—Last night a heavy sea struck the ship, and tons of water came aboard. I thought she had struck on a reef, for she trembled through every timber. The water poured down the open hatchway and drenched us. On reaching the deck, a wild scene presented itself. We were driving along over a stormy sea, which rose and fell fearfully, the ship bobbing up and down like a piece of cork on its surface. Two men were at the wheel, which required all their united strength to direct it. A full moon, occasionally hidden by the angry-looking clouds, showed us the state of the sea around us. It was a fearful sight; yet no one seemed to be afraid, everything went on as calmly as if we had a fair wind. After contemplating the scene for a time, the cold drove me back again to bed, although I did not sleep. To-day the sea has subsided, and we are going under easy canvas."

"*Dec.* 30.—Philip says we shall soon reach

Melbourne; that we have had a quick passage. We have passed several ships to-day. The roadway is thronged with passengers, as Philip said, because we are nearing the city. Indeed I hope so. It was quite hot to-day."

"*Jan.* 5.—'Land ho' early this morning. The captain was anxious to give King's Island a wide berth, several ships having been lost in that locality lately. We soon gained on the land, which had been seen from the mast-head, and passed it on our starboard. It was a rocky islet. With the help of the glass we saw several seals lying upon it, sunning themselves. We shall be at the 'Heads' by night, Philip says, and shall lie off until morning."

After the entry last quoted we entered the narrow mouth of Hobson's Bay under the guidance of a pilot, who came off to us in a little schooner, and took charge of the vessel. After entering the "Heads" we passed into a large bay, almost an inland sea, for we lost sight of the land again. A few hours, however, brought us in sight of the forest of spars which showed us the direction of the town, for beyond these were Melbourne and its suburbs. A berth at the Sandridge Pier was vacant, so we were laid up alongside by two o'clock, glad to find ourselves safe in port. The heat was terrible; the atmosphere like the breath of an oven. Everybody looked done up, and moved about with lazy steps. However, here I was at last, on the other side of the world, surprised to find so large and fine a city where, only a few years ago, there was nothing but aboriginal Mia-Mias and kangaroo.

CHAPTER IV.

BEFORE we sailed again, Philip and myself, with another sailor, got permission to go up to the gold-field town, Ballarat. We went up by train, and arrived about four o'clock in the afternoon. Here we saw holes hundreds of feet deep, out of which the precious gold was dug. These were quartz mines, and the gold was separated from the stones by heavy stampers, which could be heard beating the stones half a mile off. The gold was afterwards collected by means of quicksilver with, which it was mixed,—being then called Amalgam. The manager of one of the mines showed us several bars of amalgam weighing over three hundred pounds, one half of this being gold; and this was obtained in one week. The place where it was obtained was called Poverty Reef, by way of pleasant satire, I suppose; although one of the men told us that the claim had been worked for years before any gold had been obtained from it.

After seeing these deep mines, we were

taken to another gold-field about twelve miles off, and here the holes were not so deep,—not more than twenty feet. Here too the gold was found in the earth, not mixed with the quartz, and it was separated from the earth by being first "puddled" in a tub and then rocked in a cradle, while a plentiful supply of water was poured over the soil which was being sifted in the cradle. The fine gold was thus carried into the last compartment mixed with the finest earth. This golden sand, for such it looked, was then put into a dish and mixed with water, shaken carefully until the water, which was continually poured off, had carried every particle of the sand away, and nothing but the yellow gold remained in the bottom of the dish. There was a pound weight of gold in the dish which was shown to us after watching the various operations which I have described. This was worth about 50*l*., and was dug out by three men in less than a week.

After seeing these things, I often thought I should like to be a digger.

On our return from the diggings, we found the ship was almost ready to sail. This time she was chartered to the Chinese ports.

And thus for fully three years, Philip and I sailed together in the *Ville du Havre*, visiting all the ports in the southern hemisphere. At the end of this period he became first mate, as the captain had retired, going home to France to settle, leaving his former first mate in command of his vessel. I too had been promoted, through Philip's influence, to the poop, and was called third mate, being now twenty years old, and a good sailor, so they were kind enough to say.

At this time a little difference arose between Philip and myself which caused a separation between us for a time. He knew that I had become a Protestant, yet the fact had never occasioned any difference between us, for the change did not show itself in anything that I did; sailors have such few opportunities of being religious, and of knowing the difference which religions make among men! When any minister came on board to speak to us we all listened to him without asking whether he was Protestant or Catholic, and so it was that any change of religion did not affect the friendship of Philip and myself, until the occasion to which I now refer arose.

We had been lying in Hobson's Bay for a long time idle, for this was the dull season, and I had been allowed ashore a good deal. On the occasion of one of these holidays I consented to become a mason, and was admitted into the English Constitution. On my going on board again, I told Philip what I had done. He became angry, and said that the Catholic Church had forbidden me to become a mason.

(Philip was now more attentive to religion than he had formerly been.)

"But I do not belong to the Catholic Church, Philip. I am a Protestant, and can do as I like."

"But, Louis," he cried out angrily, "you have no right to leave the Church of your fathers, in which you were born and baptized! Dost thou not remember the little cemetery where thy father sleeps? Wouldst thou not be laid with him when thou diest?"

"My father was not a Catholic except in name, and at any rate I am now a Protestant, and intend to live and die in that faith. I am also a mason, and do not care what the priests, who are no better than ourselves, say ignorantly against the masons. They tell lies about them, I know; for all masons believe in God, and must believe in Him. Yet the priests say that the masons are atheists."

This made Philip more angry, and I do not care to write down all that my friend said to me.

At last I replied, "I will leave you, Philip; I will not stay to be spoken to in this manner."

And so I got my discharge from the *Ville du Havre*, and started for the diggings.

Soon after I had arrived at the diggings beyond Ballarat, where we had seen the men washing out the pound of gold, I saw by the papers that the *Ville du Havre* had sailed for New Caledonia, and would probably go into California before she returned to the Melbourne port.

At this I felt sad, and wished that I was with my Philip again.

Yet I would not give up being a mason, but resolved to attend all their meetings, that I might learn as much as I could about their principles.

The diggings to which I had come were altered for the worse. The gold supply was exhausted, and the diggers looked poor. Many of them were glad to work whole days for a few specks of the bright metal. So I did not stay long in this place, but moved away to a new diggings, where a great many miners were assembling. This place was called a "rush," and at first a good deal of gold was obtained by those who were fortunate enough to get "claims" on the "lead." But others who were not on the "line of gold" worked to no purpose week after week. It was very tantalizing to see men in the next hole getting gold in great quantities, washing it out of their tubs in pounds, and then to work and drive in your own hole, only a few feet away, and yet get nothing for all your pains.

At last I gave up digging and went back to Ballarat. Here, after much trouble, I got a situation as groom in a gentleman's household. And this place I got because I was a mason, for my master belonged to that order. Here I remained for more than six months. One day I saw by the papers that the *Ville du Havre* had arrived under the command of Philip Rigaud. The former captain was ill. How my heart jumped, and I resolved to go and see my old friend again; for all the anger had died out of my heart so soon as I had reached the diggings. I was to stay with my master for another week, and then I could leave. Well, before the week was up I was riding one of my master's horses in the principal street, when I saw a captain (we sailors can tell a captain by his dress and manner) driving in a cab from the railway station. I looked at him a second time, and saw that it was Philip. I rode after him and called out. He at once stopped his cab and got down, for he knew me. "I was coming to look for thee, Louis," were the first words he spoke, and regardless of by-standers, he embraced me, for I had jumped off my horse. "My heart has been sore since we parted, Louis, for I was wrong to speak to thee as I did about thy religion. Thou wilt forgive me?" It was my time to ask forgiveness for my hasty temper and hot words. And so we were reconciled. "Thou mayest remain a mason, and I will become one too, so long as I do not lose my friend." I returned with Philip to the *Ville du Havre*, and was installed as second mate, for the former second mate had left.

And now I was happy again, and determined to stick to the sea. It had been resolved to send the *Ville du Havre* on an adventurous voyage to New Guinea, for there was at this time much talk about that island. Philip was to command, for the former captain had resolved to settle in Melbourne, and I was to go as second mate. We were all in high spirits at the prospect of our voyage, for although there was some amount of danger, yet only enough to make our voyage adventurous, and we knew that we should have opportunities of making much money in trading with the natives. At the same time our pay was increased by the owners of the vessel, who did not forbid our taking little fancy things for trading purposes.

CHAPTER V.

As the step I was now taking was so full of strange consequences to myself, I like to dwell upon every event connected with it. I had, while Miss Cunningham lived, written to my mother very frequently, and had heard occasionally from her. But since my life in the southern world I had failed to write to her more than a few letters. It had been my custom, which I owed to the influence of my mistress, to send a few pounds every year to my mother. I had even done this since leaving Europe, and now that I was embarking upon what I could not help feeling was a perilous voyage, I wrote to my mother a long letter, telling her where I was going, and enclosing her 5*l*. In common with the other sailors, I took with me some rolls of bright-coloured stuffs, some tobacco and pipes, bright pieces of metal, some whistles, and other fancy things (including even dolls) which I thought would be useful in bartering with the savages. I took also

some picture-books, among which was the
"Pilgrim's Progress," given me years ago
by Miss Cunningham.

Late in the month of March we cleared
the "Heads" on our adventurous expedition.
As it was our intention to round South-East
Cape, thinking we might open out a trade
with the inhabitants of the Archipelago with
greater safety than with those of the mainland, we hugged the Australian coast until
we reached Morton Bay. We then ran due
north for several days, but had baffling
winds. The barometer began to fall rapidly;
a change in the weather was evident. At
first we thought we had escaped the equinoctial gales; but the falling of the barometer
warned us that we had not done so. As we
had still nearly six hundred miles to run, and
were anxious not to lose time, we kept on
under light canvas all the night following;
but maintained a smart look-out. Next day
the storm broke upon us, and compelled us
to lay-to, after trying to run with close-reefed
topsails. This storm tried us severely, heavy
masses of water came tumbling on board,
sweeping the decks fore and aft, and carrying off our live stock. During the day we
were exceedingly anxious, and as night
approached our anxiety increased; for the

violence of the wind was so great that we were perfectly helpless, lying like a log upon the water, which continued to make breaches over us. We all wished earnestly for the day, and when the light came the wind began to subside, so that we were now in hopes of our being able to weather the storm. Before night the water had become comparatively calm, and we began to overhaul our ship, which presented a pitiable sight. The bulwarks were smashed, the stanchions of the main cabin wrenched, and the captain's cabin broken up. The good old ship had borne up well, but she had received a severe handling. Another such storm would finish her. It was now debated whether we should return to Morton Bay and repair, or whether we should continue on our voyage after giving the vessel a slight overhaul with such appliances as we had. We determined on the latter course, as we were only five hundred miles from South-East Cape, and were all enthusiastic about our destination. I think now it would have been better if we had returned, but at that time I was—like the others—too eager to reach New Guinea to allow of the whisperings of common sense.

So all hands set to work vigorously, and in a couple of days the *Ville du Havre* looked like herself again. On the fourth day we were under sail for the Archipelago, all sanguine and hopeful. I forgot to say that one of our three boats had been smashed and carried away in the storm. Yet the two that remained were but little injured, and were soon repaired. Our glass warned us that the weather was still unsettled.

In three days we sighted a high range of mountains, which we made out to be the Owen-Stanley Mountains, running north and south from South-East Cape. This showed us that we were too much to the west to reach the Archipelago on the eastern side of the island, so we corrected our bearings, and made ourselves snug for the night. The weather looked dirty, and the glass began to fall rapidly; as the wind was from the south, and we had plenty of sea-room, and could, with such a wind, make a good offing at any time, we kept on our course under light canvas, expecting by morning to be within twenty miles of the Cape. The wind increased to a gale and blew all night without intermission. When morning broke there was a heavy sea on, the wind still rising. We were, moreover, close upon several of the islets of the Archipelago. This determined us to get away from the coast, so we put the helm up, and, turning our head east-north-east, stood away. We had not held on our new course more than an hour when the wind died away, only to begin again with renewed violence from the sou'-sou'-west. We were in a position of extreme danger, for the *Ville du Havre* had been greatly shaken by the former gale; her masts, we now found, had yielded to the severe strains which had been put on them, so we kept beating off and on all the day; but we could not get clear of the coast, the hurricane was too violent. I watched Philip's anxious face, and knew that our case was desperate unless the wind should change. Night fell, but no change came, and I now felt that our position was hopeless, for we were drifting shoreward, and had been so drifting during the day. We could see, before night fell in upon us, broken water not more than two or three miles from us. When the day closed I do not think there was a single man who expected to see the light of another day. Still we took some refreshment and stood to our posts, not knowing what chances might arise on our behalf. The dark waves rolled in upon the ship, washing our decks clean, and driving us all to shelter from the pitiless cold. The wind howled and whistled through the rigging, the ship creaked and groaned like a wounded creature, and trembled under the blows dealt by the heavy waves. I had never experienced such a storm. At this time the awful cry, so terrible to a sailor's ears, arose above the din of the elements, " Breakers on the port-bow!" We were driving helplessly on to the rocks, which were ready to engulf us. To think of anchoring was useless ; yet, as a last resource, we determined to try our anchors. Just as we were making ready, the wind began to lull; there was evidently and markedly a change. Philip now resolved to wear the ship, and gave orders to bring her about. We all sprang to our posts with renewed hope in our breasts. The ship, slowly answering to her helm, came round. It was a perilous undertaking, for we could see, even in the darkness, the white surf seething and rushing over the hidden reef. We had passed the point of danger, and began to breathe more freely, and to congratulate ourselves on our narrow escape, when a terrible shock sent the masts over the starboard, killing the first mate, and casting us all sprawling upon the deck. She had struck on another reef, and was fast embedded on the rock. Now a wild scene began. The boats were safe and ready for use, having a supply of food in them. As the sea was sweeping over the *Ville du Havre* threatening to swallow her up every moment, Philip resolved to launch the boats at once. The wind was certainly moderating, yet the sea was running mountains high. It required all the skill of our most experienced seamen, exercised under Philip's guidance, to launch our boats safely; yet this was accomplished, and they rode nobly on the wild water. As it was impossible that the ship could hold together for long, no time was lost in transferring the crew to the little boats, which rode so bravely on the water. They looked so small, and yet they were safer than the great ship, which thumped heavily every now and then on the rocks. Philip came, and, embracing me, said, "Farewell, Louis, my companion and friend; may the good God keep thee in safety. We may never meet again in this world, for I must command the one and thou the other boat. I wish thou couldst come with me, but duty separates us, my friend. Farewell;" and, kissing each other, we parted.

Philip's men were impatient, for they were ready to cast off, and as he lowered himself into the boat they cast off, the rope and were swept by the returning wave fully thirty feet from the ship. At the same instant a huge wave, all muffled in foam, came roaring and tumbling, and broke over the ship. We held on for dear life. When the water cleared Philip's boat was gone; swallowed up by the devouring sea. Our boat, too, was swept away; we were left to the mercy of the crazy hull which alone stood between us and death.

Alas, Philip, companion of my youth, and friend of my manhood! Alas, for thee! I shall see thee not again. My heart is sad, and my tears flow for thee. Soon shall I be with thee.

Such were my thoughts as I stood upon the groaning deck of the *Ville du Havre*.

The wind continued to fall rapidly. The ship, too, remained in her position. We might be safe till day broke. So at least we hoped. Five of us thus waited anxiously for the light of the day, and, as the sea subsided, began to wait hopefully. After all, we might escape. We certainly encouraged one another with the hope of escaping the fate of our companions,

CHAPTER VI.

The sun rose brilliantly over a heaving ocean. Although the wind was down, yet the sea still heaved and swelled, and its waves rolled in upon the shore with a deafening sound. The white spray almost hid the shore from our view, which was about one mile distant. A small island lay some half-mile nearer to us, and it was from this elevation that the sunken rocks on which we had struck sprang. As the ship, although at present giving us good support, was evidently breaking up, we who remained at once began to make preparations for constructing a raft. About midday we were ready, and were busy lading our raft with various necessaries, when there came upon us suddenly several canoes full of savages, and before we could offer any resistance a score of them, armed with spears, clubs, bows, and arrows, were on board. We thought it better to surrender at discretion, and were, on doing so, transferred to the canoe of one who seemed to be a chief

—a tall, black-looking negro, with hair like a mop all over his head. He was a most repulsive-looking savage. After ransacking the ship, they took the raft in tow and made for the shore. Other canoes were to be seen coming on rapidly, their crews shouting and gesticulating like maniacs. When they saw the five white men in their chief's canoe their astonishment was unbounded. Our party kept away to the north-west, and so avoided the high cliffs which we had seen from the ship. In about half an hour the chief's boat approached the mouth of a small bay which discovered itself suddenly. As we turned into this bay, I well remember how the scene which rose before us awakened within me, even in my present condition, feelings of admiration. The bay upon the south was sheltered by high hills, which sloped down to the water and were clothed thickly with timber. The western side of the bay rose gently, and spread inland in a succession of terraces. To the north the same characteristic was observable, and as the country was less thickly timbered in this direction, I could see herds of wild beasts seeking their food in the forests. The smoke arose from many places into the clear atmosphere. The bay itself was placid as a mill-pond, and shone like a mirror under the light of the sun, which was very hot. As we drew near to the shore, crowds of natives, entirely naked, ran along the beach, ready to help us to land and unload. The reader may be sure that we were in a state of great anxiety as to our fate, and sought to divine it from the faces of those around us. We had heard diverse accounts of the inhabitants of this island; some said that they were a warlike people, but capable of great generosity; others that they were unmitigated savages, even cannibals. With the last thought in our minds, we scanned every indication with deepest interest. Of course we could not know the meaning of a word that was said to us, yet we made our captors understand that we were hungry, at which some food was given us—yams, dates, and some flesh, I do not know of what kind. As the canoes were coming and going between the ship and the bay all the remainder of the day, we were handed over to the care of the women and older men, who kept guard over us and exercised their curiosity to an unlimited extent at our expense. The natives displayed great shrewdness in their attacks upon the ship's cargo, for they worked incessantly, knowing that at any moment she might disappear; and as a fact I learned afterwards, towards evening, when her balance had been disturbed by the shifting of the cargo, she suddenly careened over, and, slipping off the reef, sank in deep water, so that not a vestige of her could be seen. So suddenly had this occurred, that no warning was given to the numerous savages at work in her hold, many of whom were carried down in the *Ville du Havre*. A good many of these scrambled out of their watery prison, and, floating to the top like corks, were hauled on board the canoes of their astonished companions. Several, however, were drowned in the hold of the ship. I did not learn this for some months after it all occurred.

When night came, we were carefully confined in an empty house, consisting of two storeys, and built very neatly of wood, our hands and feet being tied to prevent us making our escape; and so we passed a miserable night, not knowing what would befall us in the morning. At sunrise several of our captors, who had slept on the ground floor (we were on the second floor), came up to see if we were safe. We made signs to them that the rope, formed from the bark of a tree, hurt us, and made them understand that we wished to be free. In a little while, the chief who had captured us was brought, and, on his giving directions to his men, our bonds were cut and we were set free. Some breakfast was brought, and we were encouraged to eat heartily. Our food consisted of fish and yams, with a pleasant drink, made, I afterwards learnt, from the leaves of a tall tree. Its taste was pungent and appetizing. In a little while we slept again, for some opiate had been put into our beverage to bring about this result. On our recovering consciousness, the sun was in the mid-heavens, and we were in a large paddock (I cannot call it by any other name), perfectly naked. We had been robbed of every vestige of clothing. A numerous crowd of savages, men, women, and children, surrounded the palisading, expressing by their gestures the astonishment, admiration, or dislike which affected the different members of the crowd. When it was seen that we were awake, some more food was brought to us, and although we did not then care to eat, yet before the day closed we were glad enough to satisfy the sharp cravings of hunger. At night we were allowed to shelter ourselves in one of the recesses of the yard, where a plentiful supply of rushes was thrown to us, just as if we were so many pigs. This treatment continued for about a week, and every day a crowd of idlers gathered about our prison to amuse themselves at our expense. They seemed to be highly amazed by our colour and general appearance, and tried to enter into conversation with us. This enabled us to learn a few words of their language. On our pointing to the sun, and showing that we would know its name, they turned their heads away, and putting up their hands in deprecation, said, "Otaroo." This, I afterwards learned, was living one, or great king, emphatically *the* living one.

As we were not molested in any other way than the manner which I have described, we began to feel at our ease, and to accept our position with cheerfulness. We ate heartily, and dismissed all concern from our minds. When our captors saw this they were evidently pleased, for they brought us a plentiful supply of food and gave us plenty of cu to drink. This, as I have said, was very appetizing, and we always ate heartily after drinking it.

At the end of a week we noticed that there were great shoutings every few hours, and, consequent upon these noises, a large increase to the crowd of watchers. This night a great noise of drums was kept up, and as soon as the day broke and the light streamed in upon our faces we found ourselves again tied hand and foot, and a guard of savages about us. They were all well armed, and had sharp flint knives. I did not like the look of our captors, and cried out to my fellow-prisoners that we were all dead men. They carried us with the greatest ease to a large open space, around which the whole population of the place was gathered. Here we were surrounded by at least a hundred armed men. A great fire was burning in the open air, which was tended by half-a-dozen stalwart savages, naked. Five large stone slabs were placed over the fire, and, judging from appearances, were as hot as the floor of an oven. Our hearts sank within us as we saw these preparations. We remembered all the stories of cannibalism we had heard, and felt that such would be our fate. A repulsive-looking man, wearing an apron of hemp (he was the priest, it appeared), came forward and examined us very carefully. He was watched intently by our guards, who were ready to obey his least wish. By his direction we were arranged in a line, according to some order; a very fat sailor, named Blewitt, on the left, I was on the extreme right. When this ceremony was finished the old man's assistants, three in number, simi-

larly attired, only in shorter aprons, stepped
forward, and began to sing or chant some
strange words. At the chorus, which was
taken up by the crowd, accompanied by the
beating of drums, two of the most powerful
of our guards seized poor Blewitt, and,
dragging him forward, threw him upon the
heated slab, at the same time striking him on
the head with a club, which rendered him
unconscious. Again the chant began, and
again, at the chorus, a second of my poor
mates was despatched in the same way as the
former sailor was destroyed. By the time
the ceremony had reached myself I was in a
kind of stupor, and was hardly conscious of
my movements. As the first strains of the
chorus arose, I put my hands up instinctively
to protect my head, and in a moment after
felt my hand grasped by the old priest. I was
conscious that he had given me the first
masonic grip. Immediately I replied, and
was answered again by him. Coming forward,
the old priest cut the rope with which my
hands and feet were bound, and, turning
himself to the crowd of astonished gazers,
addressed them, pointing now at myself, now
at the sun, and using the word "Otaroo."
Whenever this word was pronounced the
whole crowd turned away their heads, and,

putting out their hands, cried, in a subdued voice, "Otaroo!"

I was free, and was now invited to take a seat by the priest's side, and wait for my share of the horrible repast. The latter part of the invitation I declined, while accepting the former from motives of policy. I was thus constrained to sit by while the remains of my unfortunate companions were served round by the filthy cooks. The women and children were not permitted to share in the repast, which was one reserved exclusively for the warriors of the tribe.

Deeply grieved and shocked as I was at the terrible fate of my companions, yet I was filled with thankfulness at my own fortunate escape, and I could not help wondering how it had been brought about. The old priest certainly knew something of masonry, but how much knowledge he possessed, and where he had obtained it, I cannot say. I know only that his knowledge was the means of saving my life, and of inducing him to treat me with kindness. I was now permitted to go about freely, and was taken by the priest to his house. I thus became sacred, and my safety was secured at least for a time.

The priest's house was different in many respects from the houses of the other chiefs.

It was larger, and consisted of three floors, one of which was dug out of the earth. Into this room no person was permitted to enter but the priest himself. The second floor, level with the street, consisted of only one very large room, twelve feet by twenty, which had no connection with either the upper or lower storey. The upper storey, divided into three compartments, was occupied by the priest's wives, one in each compartment. In this respect he differed from the other savages, who were only permitted to have one wife. A distinguished chief was permitted to have two, and was expected to have two rooms on the upper storey. The commoner people lived wholly on a ground floor. Many of the houses had verandahs round them, sometimes on both upper and lower storeys.

But this was a privilege that was not permitted to the smaller houses, unless their occupants had distinguished themselves in some way. The fact is that the storeys and compartments of a man's house, together with the style of the verandah, were a mark of his position in his tribe. At one glance you could tell who among the people of the village were the principal and who the inferior people. The village of Rágek consisted of about fifty or sixty houses, and was delightfully situated, affording opportunities for hunting and fishing during the greater portion of the year. Here I remained for several months, and made great progress in speaking the language. By this means I picked up considerable information about the interior, and heard many wonderful reports of its mysteries, which awakened in me the desire to penetrate the dense forests which sheltered it, and reach the kingdom of K'ootar enclosed within the high ranges, whose peaks of snow I had seen when on a hunting expedition some ten miles inland, from the higher ground.

CHAPTER VII.

As the reader may learn from the closing sentence of the last chapter, I was allowed the exercise of a great deal of liberty, indeed was perfectly unrestrained, sharing freely in all the expeditions of the tribe for hunting or fishing purposes. On one of these expeditions inland we reached a very high hill—part of a range of mountains, running north and south.

As I was anxious to obtain some idea of the country beyond, I persuaded my companions to ascend the range with me, and on reaching the top I was able to see the summits of a distant mountain, or range of mountains, whose whitened peaks were lost in the clouds. On inquiring the name of this mountain the natives shook their heads, and became silent. After much persuasion on my part they told me that it belonged to the kingdom of K'ootar, and that a great king ruled over the surrounding country. His power was so great that none of the chiefs, nor even the priests on the coast country, were able to stand against him. I could get very little information about this inland tribe, as my companions did not care to speak about the kingdom of K'ootar, being fearful of the vengeance of the mountaineers. The fact is many of them had a superstitious belief that their words were carried to these terrible people by invisible spirits. Hence they spake only in whispers about the Great Kingdom in Tanna-Vorkoo (the mountain range). I had heard enough, however, to excite my imagination, and to prepare me for adventure. Part of the information that I thus gathered was this. The people inhabiting the mountain sometimes came down to the coast, riding on evil spirits which moved like the wind, breathing out fire from their nostrils, and that nothing could withstand them. The horsemen who rode on these fierce spirits were clothed with flames, and burnt up everything like the sun, dazzling the eyes of all who looked upon them. From this I made out that these mountain men were well armed, and had bright, perhaps golden armour; for one of the prevailing stories in Australia before we started was that the interior of the country was rich in gold.

Although much that was told me about the

Orangwŏks (for such was their name) was utter folly, yet I felt sure that there was some foundation in fact, for these exaggerated reports, and by some curious circumstances I was able to make out the truth about the mountain tribe.

The priest (whose name was Lakangéoo) had taken me to live in his house, for a reason which will presently appear, and I obtained through his favour the restoration of my clothes, with those of my poor mates who had been murdered. I obtained also some of the things which had been stolen from the ship. Amongst these were some books, a Bible, the old "Pilgrim's Progress," and some pictures. I got also some pencils, and a few quires of foolscap paper, which were very useful to me. But to return. The "Pilgrim's Progress" was, as the reader may remember, illustrated; and among the illustrations was a highly-coloured picture of Christian on the Delectable Mountains. On the plain was a flock of sheep, several of which were brought out towards the foreground. After my conversation about the kingdom of K'ootar, I was showing these pictures to one of the natives who had given me the information about the evil spirits ridden by the mountaineers, and when we came to the picture of the sheep on the Delectable Mountains, he exclaimed, "Ahzĕ, ahzĕ,"—evil spirit, evil spirit, and pointed to the sheep. I understood from this that the mountain tribe were possessed of horses, or ponies.

Lakangéoo (the priest) was a very shrewd man, and endeavoured to obtain from me information that might be useful to himself. He, I suspect, fully understood that white men were superior to black men. From words that fell from him from time to time, I came to the conclusion that many years ago he had been in possession of a white man, and I suspected that the priest's knowledge of masonry was derived from his white prisoner, as he often made inquiries about European practices (in these inquiries he betrayed the existence of a previous knowledge). I related incidents of my own life, and among them I told him of my digging experiences. The old man's eyes twinkled as he listened to me, and his manner became eager as I told him that the metal which was thus dug out of the earth was the same as that used by the mountain chiefs in their dress and shields; and showing him a highly-coloured picture in the "Pilgrim's Progress," where a bright yellow colour was conspicuous, I illustrated my meaning to him. After this he was always ready to talk to me about the way the English gold-miner obtained the precious metal from the earth. From the persistency with which he dwelt on the idea, I knew he had some plot in his head, and felt sure that a short time would reveal what it was. So one day, after renewing our conversation about the way of procuring gold, Lakangéoo said to me,—

"There is gold in K'ootar dug out of the mountains in large quantities."

"So I thought," was my reply; "do the Orangwöks work their mines?"

"Yes, after a fashion. We could show them how to work them to greater advantage."

"But would they not kill us if we crossed the great Tannavorkoo?" for so was the mountain called.

He replied, with an expression of contempt, "If we can show them how to work their mines, they will welcome us. I have lived many suns," he said, pointing to his white hair, as one might appeal to one's knowledge of the world.

From this time he began to plan with me an adventure into the K'ootar territory. I was as eager, although from a different motive, as Lakangéoo, and resolved to share the adventure with him; so, giving out that he was going to confer with Otaroo, he and myself, accompanied by six strong men as an escort, carrying all that we considered valuable, started, taking a north-east route. Under the guidance of the old priest, we skirted the ground of other tribes that lay between ourselves and the frontier, which, after three days' travelling, we reached in safety. The land had been gradually rising since we left the coast; now it suddenly fell some hundreds of feet, making a natural rampart like a precipice some hundreds of feet deep. Before descending the precipitous rampart, I will describe the view which we now saw. A vast plain, well-watered, well-wooded, well-cultivated. Streams of water ran through all its extent, rendering it wonderfully fertile. These streams discharged themselves into a lake at the foot of the natural rampart which bounded the kingdom of K'ootar. The lake had (as far as I could learn) no outlet, so I conclude the water escaped by some subterranean channel, so passing on to the sea, and, as some believed, fertilizing the coast country, in its underground progress. The whole of this immense plain was under cultivation, and was like the garden of Eden for beauty and fertility. Even now I could see through the clearings evidences of cultivation. The rising smoke, curling high above the tall palm-trees, showed in places innumerable the presence of habitation—herds of cattle, buffalo or bison, antelopes, and other game were to be seen in all directions. As we went through this natural paradise, we saw richly plumaged birds, in size and variegated colours such as I had never imagined. These birds were called wawkoo.

Beyond all, about fifty miles distant, a very high mountain rose, and had its highest snow-capped peaks in the clouds; this was the range called Tannavorkoo. It spread itself out far beyond the limits of my vision, maintaining everywhere its altitude. It was such a range as might bar the progress of the inexperienced traveller, and turn him back to the fertile plain, out of which it rose. I had not the least suspicion at this time that there was a habitable, still less that there was an actually inhabited territory, in the midst of this range of high hills.

Before descending to the plain, we sent back our escort, who had scarcely dared to look out over K'ootar territory. It would have been instant death to any one of them to set his foot in that plain, so at least said Lakangóoo.

F

No sooner had the priest and myself descended, carrying our luggage with us, than as if from the ground, a score of Orangwöks enclosed us. They were mounted on little ponies, striped with yellow and white, which moved with great speed. Their riders were clothed in a long, loose-fitting robe, reaching below the knee; this was the common dress of the country. They were armed with swords, spears, and bows and arrows. Some of them carried shields of pure gold, and others had a breastplate of gold bars. They had a warlike look, although they were of small stature. We were seized before we had time to offer resistance, even had we thought of doing so, and bound with a well-made rope of bark and gold thread.

The head of the troop demanded our names and business in a tone of authority. He spoke the same language as the coast tribe, but spoke it differently. The coast tribe spoke from the throat; the Orangwöks spoke from their lips and upper part of the mouth; their voice too was more resonant, their pronunciation of the words was also different, and many of the words used were unknown to me. Lakangéoo replied to the speaker, and explained in an undertone our business. The officer listenened with an indifferent air

THE CAPTURE.

Page 66.

until the priest mentioned the goldmines. The chief's attention was at once aroused, and he now displayed the keenest interest. When the priest finished speaking, at a word from the leader, every Orangwŏk sheated his sword, or lowered his spear, from which I inferred that we were safe, and prepared to ride onward. Our course lay along a well-made, well-beaten road; the officer at the head of the troop having first sent on two of his soldiers (I suppose I must call them such) in the direction of the mountain range of which I have spoken. Their little ponies went like the wind, and their white and yellow stripes flashed in the passing light in a striking manner; so too did the arms and shields, which were brightly burnished. I could now understand how the imagination of the coast natives had been wrought upon by the vision of some hundreds of the Orangwŏks riding rapidly in their bright armour.

CHAPTER VIII.

Lakangéoo and myself were still carrying the heavy bundles containing our valuables, which had hitherto been borne by our escort. These packages weighed upwards of fifty pounds each, and under a hot sun, for it was now past noon, we found the burden as heavy as we could well bear at the rapid pace we were travelling, for, of course, there were no ponies for us. After an hour's quick walking we reached a well-constructed house built on the side of the road, and surrounded by waving trees, very tall and graceful, which sheltered the building from the great heat. We were glad of the rest which we were allowed to take at this place; some refreshments had been prepared for us, ordered by the couriers who had been sent on in advance, and who, it appeared, still continued in advance of us all along the route. The house was the finest-looking one I had yet seen. It was built of wood throughout, and the rooms were very capacious. There were underground rooms for summer use, and two stories above. Although the wood-work was generally of a rough description, yet there were indications of a better taste in the carved finishings, and the worked pillars supporting the verandah which here, as on the coast, ran all round the house, both upstairs and down. The upstair rooms were reached on the outside by a well-made ladder. The yard in which this house was built was surrounded by tropical vegetation and tropical fruits. In one corner of the court was a fine bath, sheltered by trees. This was the first bath I had seen, and I was glad to avail myself of the permission to have a swim in the water, which I found delightfully cool. A magnificent specimen of the wawkoo sat in one of the tall trees, watching my bathing operations. Its feathers, which were of gold, crimson, blue, of every colour of the rainbow, shone richly in the sun. The note of the bird is, however, very coarse and unmusical.

After a rest of a couple of hours our captors prepared to continue their march. The priest and myself were now placed upon horseback—that is, we were put upon little ponies such as our captors rode. This was a great relief to me, especially as our burdens had been strapped upon another pony. When all was ready we were placed in the middle, four riding in advance, four on either hand, and the remainder of the troop bringing up the rear. At the word "blanputt" we started at a rapid pace, a quick canter, which soon quickened to a hand-gallop, as our little ponies got warm, and thus we continued for a full hour, the horses' feet, with the spears and swords of our escort, making a great clatter.

The Orangwöks—judging from our guards, and I found that they were good specimens of the tribe generally—were short, not more than five feet in height, some of them as little as four feet six. They were fairer than the coast natives, and had straight hair. In many there was a tendency to curl at the ends, and in some few there was an actual frizziness all over the head. They were very proud of their hair and their teeth, which were pearly white. In this there was a striking contrast with the shore tribe, whose hair stood up like a huge mop, or like porcupine quills, all round the head, and whose teeth were often very offensive. An Orangwök reminded me of a Malay, and yet he was something like a negro too, but very much superior to the ordinary Papuan.

While I make these reflections we are galloping along the great highway, every few miles passing a house like the one at which we had rested. These houses were placed every ten or twelve miles, and were posting houses for the king's service. Once we met a troop of horsemen passing eastward, a short parley ensued, the priest and myself were examined, in much the same way as indolent men would examine some curious specimen, with a mixture of indifference, contempt, and curiosity, and then on we went again. At night we rested in one of the posting-houses, and were off again at sunrise. I was in great agony, for I had not ridden for nearly twelve months, and the priest was in a worse condition. Still we were hurried on, until towards noon we approached the foot of the great Tannavorkoo. We now halted at the last posting-house on the plain, and had some refreshments.

About four o'clock we mounted our ponies again, and began to ascend the range. I was surprised to find so good a road cut out of the solid rock. Places which seemed inaccessible, had been reached, great blocks of stone broken away, and a good roadway cleared. We continued to rise until night fell; even now we did not draw rein, but kept on at a quick pace for an hour, until I could no longer see the road, which I knew was not more than eight or ten feet wide in places. We now reached a small posting-house, and remained there for the night. Early in the morning we were again on our way, after taking a look at the road which we had passed over in the dark. We had been travelling along the edge of a precipice which fell away from the parapet abruptly, and had a descent of nearly 1000 feet. When we had reached an altitude of about 3000 feet above the level of the plain, we entered a vast plateau clothed with some tropical vegetation, and very fertile, we saw the smoke of a town or village before us, and were glad to hurry on and rest ourselves, for I thought that now our journey was over. Some ten or twelve miles farther inland the land began to rise again, and form a new base for Tannavorkoo whose peaks seemed to reach to the clouds. It was evident that we were still at the base of the great mountain. We rested at this village, or town, the first that I had seen of the Orangwöks, but as I shall have opportunity to describe the capital city, I need not stay to describe this, which was only a town of about three thousand inhabitants. I was much struck by the evidences of superior civilization which it presented.

After a few hours' rest, I learned to my regret that we had still to travel onward, and upward. This plateau was for spring habitation, and it was now the height of summer. It was well-watered by a river, which descended from the mountain range, and which was judiciously directed into numerous channels or canals. The danger incident to mountain torrents or rivers was thus avoided, and the whole land was fertilized by the general diffusion of the water. As we neared the defile of the upper Tannavorkoo, a horseman started out and challenged us. On receiving our pass-word he allowed us to enter the defile. As we entered, I saw the shields and spears of a troop of horse, who were guarding the approaches, rising out of a plantation. A handful of men could keep such a pass against thousands. Another day's travelling brought us to the higher plateau of the kingdom of K'ootar, where the king and his warriors have their summer residence. As we rose to the level of the plain we felt the agreeable change in the atmosphere. Every man, as we ascended to the level country, lifted his head-gear, which consisted of a light frame of bamboo, covered with neat grass-work. I thought that this was some religious act, but I learnt that it was an act of homage to the king, whose sacred presence filled the whole plain. We now moved on more quietly, although we still moved quickly. As we neared the city every man again took off his head-gear, and after mumbling some words replaced it on his head. On entering the city every one became silent, or spoke only in whispers. This, I was informed, was out of respect for the king's palace, which was inside the city; and here I may mention that it was not considered good manners to speak above a whisper while inside the walls of K'ootar (the city gave its name to the kingdom). It was this restriction which doubtless formed that habit of restraint and silence which was so observable in the Orangwŏks, especially when contrasted with the Papuans proper, who were a highly excitable and boisterous people. We walked the streets in silence, having dismounted. Our coming did not apparently occasion any surprise on the part of the inhabitants. No one turned to look at us; and those who passed us only noticed us by turning up the palms of their hands, and looking into it, their mode of salutation.

CHAPTER IX.

K'ootar consisted of about two thousand or three thousand houses, and had a population of nearly ten thousand people. It was by far the finest city of the kingdom, though by no means the largest. None but chiefs and warriors were permitted to *live* in K'ootar, although any person, on receiving permission, was allowed to stay in it for a limited time. The houses were of several storeys, varying from three (including the ground floor) to seven. The palace of the king consisted of seven storeys. A few of the more distinguished chiefs had houses of six storeys, others less distinguished had five, four, or three. No house of less than three was allowed to be built in K'ootar. This procured a uniformity which was very agreeable to the eye. The streets were narrow—the only fault I could find with the style of the city—so narrow, that one's movements were considerably impeded if one was in a hurry.

As, however, nobody was permitted to hasten or appear hurried in K'ootar, this inconvenience was not felt. The houses were verandahed as on the coast, but more elaborately, and with greater regard to the rank and distinction of the possessor. The palace had a verandah running right round the house on each storey. In many of the chiefs' houses these verandahs did not go completely round. It was a point of etiquette rigidly enforced that no verandah could be added on any pretence whatever, without the express sanction of the king, who even held a consultation with his wise men, the ŭŏŏ, before granting it. A description of one of these houses will suffice for all.

The house at which I was lodged, until the king's pleasure respecting me was known, consisted of two large rooms on the ground floor, each fifteen feet by twenty; out of one of these rooms there was an approach by means of a ladder to the upper storey, which again consisted of two rooms. Above this storey were two other storeys, but the lower one was reached from the outside from a courtyard by means of a carved ladder, which had a balustrade running down one side of it. From this third storey the top floor was reached from within. This was the floor of honour, and the two upper storeys were reserved for the women of the family. There was little or no furniture in our sense of the term. Well-carved settles were placed round each room, which were used as both seats and beds. The floor was covered with well-wrought mats, and the walls were decorated with bright-coloured feathers and skins. The meals were taken in the second storey, the members of the family in the upper rooms coming down to take part in the common meal. After all the family had seated themselves on mats or rushes, a slave brought the food on clean leaves or well-scoured marble dishes, according to the nature of the food. When many guests were present, and it was desired to honour them, a different method was observed in serving the dinner or breakfast, for there was no evening meal. Each room had a large opening in the centre of the floor, which was skilfully concealed under ordinary circumstances, but, on the occasion to which I refer, these openings were exposed, and the guests and members of the family sat round them chatting and laughing. Presently the head of a slave would appear above the opening, and then his shoulders, until his waist was on a level with the floor. He had in his hand the supply of food, which was handed about by him in a remarkably quick manner, for it is not considered etiquette for one guest to handle the food of another. The slave had to move all round the opening, serving each guest with whatever he required. This was managed by an apparatus set up on the lower storey, by which means he was enabled to walk rapidly round the inside of the table so to speak. At least one other slave, was kept waiting upon the slave who was serving the guests. It was considered a mark of distinction to be invited to dine with a chief who required three or four slaves to serve his guests. In the houses of the chiefs who were able to do this, the dining-room would be on the third or fourth storey. That of the king was on the fifth floor, and full a dozen slaves were kept upon his dining-ladder. It seemed to me that the most difficult and unpleasant thing to do was considered the most honourable by this people. But it is time to return from this digression, as I do not doubt the reader is equally anxious as myself to know how I am to be received by the king. At first I was lodged, or placed in custody of an old chief, of moderate distinction, who had a three-storeyed house.

Lakangéoo was placed in charge of some

other chief. Old Kayhar, the chief with whom I was placed, had one wife and a daughter about fifteen, the latter being evidently in delicate health. They were all very kind to me, and entered into conversation, inquiring how I became white, and whether there was any other country than K'ootar, except the country of the Kahshi—coarse spirits—the coast tribes. These Papuans were universally called Kahshi by the Orangwöks, and no greater term of contempt or offence was known among them. I replied by telling them of Europe, and describing its great cities, its fleets of ships, the grandeur of its kings. At this they were all silent. They evidently did not believe me, yet were unwilling to contradict what I said. As they all left the room that night, they raised their hands, and, turning up the palm as if they would examine it, bade me good night.

Here was I in such a position as probably no European had ever been in before. I thought my life was safe, yet I was too excited to sleep. My mind revelled in the idea of adventure, and I gave full play to my imagination.

In about a fortnight a great chief, who had been brought from a distant part of the kingdom, arrived, and, after repeated conferences with him, the king decided that I should be admitted to his presence. It appears that Lakangéoo had been interrogated about me, and had revealed our knowledge of gold-mining to my captors. The chief who had been brought from a distance had been in charge of the gold-mining operations. Hence the reason of his coming. He had conferred with me several times before it had been decided that I should be presented to the king. Once having seen him, my kind host's daughter told me, my life was safe. Lakangéoo had not been permitted to see him; and here I may say that I never again saw the old priest, nor do I know what became of him. I never could obtain a scrap of information respecting his fate. The day I was presented was ushered in by the beating of drums, the blowing of horns, and the jingling of a small instrument made of gold bars. The sounds made were very pleasing, but I am not able to say how far they were musical.

At sunrise the town was astir, for the day was a gala day, and people poured into the streets from the country. Dressed in their best, I was going to write, but this would be a misnomer. They were nearly naked, having only a thin piece of well-wrought stuff descending from the loins to the knees. The men who were permitted to enter the palace courtyard, had on only a short strip of thin stuff, not more than six inches long. The women who took part in the proceedings of the palace were perfectly naked, with the exception of a few ornaments. This was to me a disgusting and immodest exposure; and yet the women themselves did not seem to think there was any immodesty in their dress, or want of dress. What makes this the more noticeable is the fact that ordinarily they are decently covered, and are generally a remarkably modest class of women.

During the time I was lodging with Kayhar I had learnt, if not to speak like the Orang-wŏks, yet to understand their pronunciation. For a time I was very much puzzled by their speech, which was not at all like that of the Kahshi. The sound was loud and resonant, and appeared to come from a distance. Even in K'ootar itself the whispers were marked by the same characteristic; they seemed to come from the top of the speaker's head. I had got somewhat accustomed to this in my host's family, and could now readily understand their speech, although many of their words were still unknown to me. I had been carefully instructed in the etiquette connected with a presentation by my host, so I did not fear the ceremonies of the coming day. Indeed I was most anxious to see the terrible king, of whom everybody stood in such awe. I had thought that there was something special about this particular levée, if I may call the ceremony of a savage court by such a name—that it was specially convened in connection with myself. This was not the case, however. It was the regular assembly held every month, except in the winter, on the day of the full moon. The presentations were made in a spacious courtyard, reserved for state occasions. The floor of this yard was of marble, inlaid with bars of gold. The marble was smooth and well polished, but the gold was rough and frosted. In the centre of the floor was a daïs, very roomy, and on the daïs were two thrones raised by means of several steps considerably above the level of the daïs itself. The thrones were of pure gold, and were surrounded by brightly-polished mirrors, which caught and reflected the sun's light in a most dazzling manner. Indeed one could not look without blinking at the king and his wife, who occupied the thrones. On the first step on either side of the king stood one of the ŭŏŏ men with long grey hair and beard; below them, on the next step, stood two more of the ŭŏŏ, younger in years, while the daïs was occupied by a troop of guards, who surrounded the sacred steps. Immediately on either side of the thrones, but standing on the daïs, were two immense tigers, beautifully striped. They looked as if they were ready to spring upon the prostrate crowd of courtiers, but they were firmly secured by means of well-wrought ropes, twisted with gold wire. The whole yard was lined with guards who sat upon their little ponies against the wall, and, with couched spears or drawn swords, looked as if they were only waiting for a nod from the despot to fall upon the crowd and slay them. Every one who entered passed up a lane of such guards, and on approaching the daïs fell upon his stomach, drawing himself along in this position until he was opposite the king's throne. He then turned up his hand towards the king three times, keeping his face to the ground all the time, and on receiving a gentle prick from the spear of one of the many guards, he moved on again until he got beyond the limits of the daïs. On reaching this limit, he sprang to his feet, and, entering the crowd of spectators who were in the galleries around the courtyard, took his place among the onlookers. Although the ceremonies were very painful, yet they were performed with great rapidity, as one person followed quickly upon the heels of another. Nearly five hours, however, elapsed before my turn came to be presented. I was neither courtier nor criminal—a kind of suitor for mercy; so my case was peculiar. When I came opposite the throne I stopped, and was questioned amid the breathless silence of the crowd.

"What is your name?"

"Trégan." (My sailor friends had shortened my name to Trigg—sometimes Trik—but the Kahshi had called me Trégan, which suited the genius of their language, so I gave my name as Trégan.)

"What country did you come from?"

"A country beyond the great ocean."

After this answer there was a short silence, and some consultation.

"How did you become white?"

"I was born so. All people are white in my country."

At this there was another short silence, and a further consultation. I heard the word "ĕdzĕ" used several times. I was afraid I was getting into disgrace again.

"What do people in your country do?"

"Dig gold out of the earth."

"How is the gold obtained?"

To this I replied shortly by explaining.

"Will you go to the gold-mines of the Great King?" (And here I could feel there was a general movement of reverence.) " And teach his servants to get gold?"

To this I replied that I would.

These questions were not put to me by the king himself. He addressed the wise man on his right hand, who again communicated with one on the next step, and he to one on the daïs. My answer was conveyed to the king after a similar manner, but going the reverse way, being delivered to him by the wise man on his left hand.

I was now gently touched with the spear, and moved on, pleased that the wearisome and painful exhibition was over. On going up into the galleries already mentioned, I was struck with the magnificence of the ceremonial. The bright sun, which fell upon the gorgeous spectacle, illuminated the vast court with dazzling light; for every guard was clothed in bright uniform overlaid with gold. Everywhere there was a profusion of this metal.

The king was very small, not more than four feet high, and made in proportion. His wife was still smaller. They were richly dressed, and their jewels (they were the only persons permitted to wear jewels) shone with a dazzling lustre. In addition to the tigers I have mentioned there were on the outer rim of the daïs four wild-looking animals (bisons, I believe they were); while in the trees which shaded the throne, and which were carefully cultivated, there sat several magnificent wawkoo.

As the king and the queen descended from their high seat the crowd prostrated themselves, and so remained until their Majesties had withdrawn. The ceremony, to which so many looked forward with eager anxiety, had now come to an end, and we were free to return to our houses. I may mention here that no sooner had the king withdrawn than I was surrounded by an eager throng of Orangwök warriors, their wives and daughters, who saluted me, and welcomed me to K'ootar, pressing invitations to visit them at their houses upon me. It seemed as if I was in a charmed world.

On my return to the house of Kayhar I was welcomed very heartily by Lamlam, my host's daughter, who was eager to know what I thought of the great ceremony. I expressed my admiration and wonder at the splendour which I had seen, which gratified my fair questioner. I could not help, however, remarking upon the women's want of costume on such occasions. Lamlam seemed surprised at this, and said,—

"It is usual; everybody does it. Where is the harm in it?"

"It is not done in my country," I replied. "Any woman who acted so would be looked upon with abhorrence as indecent."

This hurt the gentle Lamlam, so I hastened to explain that probably habit made all the difference between the usages of different people.

"Yes," she replied, "we are accustomed to this practice from the time we are children, and no one refuses to conform to it except those who are ĕdzĕ (that is, out of their mind), and they are sent out of K'ootar. No one is permitted to live here who does not conform to our customs."

CHAPTER X.

HOTARWŏKOO,[1] for such was the name of the king of K'ootar, meaning the living one—terrible king of beauty—such, at least, is the nearest approach that can be made in English to the meaning of the name—Hotarwŏkoo was about thirty years old. He had succeeded the previous king five years before, and had been selected to succeed by a council of the üŏŏ. It appears from what I could learn that the eldest son of the king does not necessarily succeed his father to the throne. The heir is elected by the council of wise men, who meet in secret, in a darkened chamber, for the purpose of designating the king's succesor. He must belong to one of the principal families, and must not be more than four feet high; for such is one of the absurd restrictions imposed upon the choice

---

[1] The frequent recurrence of the vowels *oo* in combination has led me to the conclusion that they have an adjective force; and that they are equivalent to *good*, or *great*.—ED.

of the ŭŏŏ. I could not ascertain how or when this restriction was first imposed, but suspect that it was a device of the chieftains in an earlier age to protect themselves and their families from the mere brute force of their superior chief. But however the practice arose, it is certain that no one now questions its expediency. Yet it had a very bad effect upon the physical training of the Orangwöks, for it set a kind of fashion of smallness, which had an injurious effect upon the people generally; at any rate, upon the chiefs. The present king had the reputation of being an amiable man, and was held in very high regard in consequence. I do not know that he ever distinguished himself in any way, but as the kingdom was prosperous, and had been long at peace, much of this favourable condition of things was ignorantly attributed to him; and as he did not mix with the nobles (if I may call them by a name which is so misleading), and lived in a very secluded manner, he was held in greater awe, as well as affection, than any of his predecessors, I was assured. I have several times spoken of his wife. I should have mentioned his wives, for he had seven; only, six of them were not supposed to be known, nor were they ever spoken of in the presence of the wives and daughters of the other chiefs. These wives were never seen in public, and nobody knew anything about them. Here is a fitting place to mention the usages of the Orangwŏk nobles respecting wives. Polygamy was allowed, but was not encouraged. The women, I was glad to learn, were entirely opposed to it, except in very exceptional cases. No chief, however, was permitted to have more than four wives, and they, like the additional wives of the king, were not generally known. It is not to be supposed that many of the chiefs really had so many as four wives, for such was not the case. For every separate wife a chief was bound, by strict custom, to build and maintain a separate establishment. This fact naturally tended to hinder the growth of polygamy.

As it is not my intention, even if I had the ability or knowledge which would enable me to do so, to write a book about the customs and habits of the people of K'ootar, I will return from this digression to my own personal adventures while in this country. As I have said, I was heartily welcomed by Kayhar and his family on my return from the palace, and was treated with great kindness. A room was now assigned me for my own sole use until it was decided when I was to start for the king's mines. I had also my clothing restored to me, together with several of the books and the paper which had been saved from the wreck. Both books and paper were a great source of comfort to me. The pictures were intensely amusing to Lamlam, and when she saw me reading off the page of the book a real story, which I translated as well as I could as I read, she was excessively astonished, and called her mother to witness this marvellous feat. After seeing these things, and seeing me use the pencil for the purpose of drawing in a rude way some figures, they began to question me more minutely about the great world beyond the sea. Next morning, Lamlam came to me, and begged me to teach her to speak to the wonderful book. I explained, after reading the English aloud, that it would be impossible for her to understand it; but I would teach her to write with the pencil. So apt was she that before the day closed she had learnt several words, quite a dozen, off by heart. The characters were of course English, but the words spelt were Orangwŏk words. I then wrote them in the order of a sentence, which she read aloud with childish delight. This was the sentence I composed for her:—

"Pretty Lamlam has asked Trégan to

teach her. Trégan will teach Lamlam to read. Lamlam is pretty and good."

Having read this over again, making out each word slowly, she ran to her mother, and showing her what she had on the paper, read it aloud. Every day after this, she came to me to give her a lesson, which I gladly did.

I had a natural talent for drawing, and although I had not cultivated it, yet I could draw anything that I saw roughly in outline. One day I took a rough sketch of Tannavorkoo, and showed it to Lamlam. This again amazed her, for these people, though not wanting in ability, yet had no literature of any kind, and made no attempt, beyond a little carving, to imitate the works of nature. They would say, "If you want a wawkoo keep one in your house." I then, while Lamlam sat patiently, tried to make a sketch of her face. After a sort I caught its expression, and then gave the drawing to her. Situated as I was, I resolved to endeavour to improve myself in every way that I could. I felt that this would relieve the tediousness of my captivity, for such I began to feel my position to be. I often walked out with Kayhar to see the city. The character of the houses has been described. Behind them there ran in every case a large garden-plot—

in some cases very large—kept like a park. This park had in it rare trees and flowers, beautiful specimens of the birds of the country, and an abundant supply of tropical fruits. Nearly every chief kept a slave, whose sole business it was to play some musical instrument, generally a drum. This was accompanied by a shrill instrument, made from a bamboo reed. Occasionally, the more distinguished chiefs added a third of gold bars, and so formed a small band, which played of an afternoon in the garden-parks. As these garden-parks were attached to every chief's house, K'ootar covered a very large extent of ground.

After I had been idle for about three weeks longer, I was warned that in seven days (the day after the monthly levée) I must start for the king's mines. I at once signified my readiness to start whenever his Majesty should be pleased to direct me to do so.

I left some of my pencils and paper (indeed the greater portion of the latter) with Lamlam; I left her also the illustrated "Pilgrim's Progress," and the pictures. I took with me my Bible—the present of my dear mistress—some pencils, and a few quires of foolscap paper.

When the time drew near for me to leave

the house of my kind host, I felt very heavy and sorrowful. I had become quite attached to the whole family.

As I was to leave in the morning at four o'clock, just as the sun rose, I bade my kind friends good-bye (English fashion) by shaking hands overnight, and then retired to rest. At four o'clock I was ready to start, and was preparing to leave the door-way, when little Lamlam entered. The tears stood in her eyes, as she gave me her hand and bade me good-bye again. I was much touched with this instance of her affection, and could not resist the impulse to bid her farewell Frenchwise, telling her I would often think of Lamlam.

CHAPTER XI.

Our party consisted of the old chief, who was governor of the mining territory Wătárá, and who was accompanied on his return to that district by several other chiefs, a company of not less than twenty guards, several —not fewer than six—criminals (these were picked up about ten miles from K'ootar), and myself. We were all mounted on ponies, and the guards were well armed. The old chief and his companions formed a party of their own, so the officer in command of the troop invited me to ride by his side, an invitation which I very gladly accepted. The sun was already showing like a ball of fire above the eastern hills, when we started from the gate of K'ootar. The rays of the sun were shining clearly and strongly on the snowy tops of Tannavorkoo, dispersing the light mists which hung around its brow. Even now the heat was great, but our quick motion created a pleasant breeze, which kept us beautifully cool. At a distance of ten miles we reached a small outpost, consisting of several guard-houses. Here we took up our contingent of criminals, for persons under sentence for any crime were not allowed to come within ten miles of K'ootar. I found now that all criminals were sentenced to work at the mines. And once there it was not often that they returned to K'ootar proper. They might collect sufficient gold at Wătárá to redeem their liberty; and on doing this they were in a position to return, of whatever crime they had been convicted, short of treason against the king. The Orangwŏks did not appear to have any idea of the immoral nature of crime. Crime was to them simply a violation of the laws or usages of their land. It did not leave behind it any moral taint, which would prevent the person who had recovered his liberty (very few ever did redeem themselves, I found) from returning to his old place among his friends.

After baiting our hardy little ponies—for we had a long day's ride before us—we started again, the prisoners in the centre of the troop. As I rode by the side of the officer of the troop, named Lanna, I entered into conversation with him respecting the nature of the prisoners' offences. There was one of the criminals, who had a very repulsive appearance, sullen and cruel-looking. I asked my companion the nature of his offence.

"He," was the reply, "committed murder, and stole the murdered man's property. He escaped to the mountains, and defied all our attempts to take him. He was caught at last by a clever stratagem."

"What was its nature?" I asked.

"Well, it was known that he was very fond of his son, a boy of about fourteen years old, very small in stature, so our chief," he said, lifting his hat, "sent for the youth, and had him kept in close quarters until a powerful man of the youth's size could be discovered. This was a work of some difficulty, for strength requires size." (At this my friend swelled his little body out to its full dimensions.) At last a very small man was found who was extremely powerful. The fact is, there is not a man in our troop, and we have some very powerful men" (again my friend inflated himself) "among us, who was able to hold him or throw him, and what was of more importance, was able to get out of his clutches when once in them. Now, the boy was very pale, and had a limp in his left leg, so our chief procured a skilful imitator, and directed him to make the little man like the murderer's son. This was not easily done, yet all things yielded to skill and patience, and at last the boy was brought into the presence of our chief. 'Well, my boy,' he said, ' so you wish to return to your home ?'

"' If you will graciously allow me to do so,' was the reply.

" The chief started. He had been deceived by the striking likeness to the murderer's son.

" This man was now sent to the mountains, and shortly found himself in the embrace of yonder villain. You may imagine the scoundrel's surprise to find that his beloved son grasped him so firmly, and that by no effort could he succeed in freeing himself from that iron grasp. At first he thought his son was ëdzĕ. But when he learned the fact that he was actually in the hands of his enemies his rage knew no bounds. It was a clever trick," continued the young officer, laughing heartily at his recollection of the stratagem.

" And can that man return again to the society of innocent people after a time ? How many years is he sentenced to remain at the mines ?"

" He may never come back again. The

probability is that he will turn scoundrel there, and die at the mines. He is not sent for any particular time, only until he has raised a certain amount of gold. The time he takes to do this will depend upon his luck as well as his skill and industry. And when he has done this, why shouldn't he return to K'ootar? He is not worse than others. All men have murder in their hearts."

"And who is that young man, with rather a pleasant, intelligent-looking face, who is bound with the murderer?"

"He is a worse character still. You see how you may be deceived by a man's face."

"What did he do, then? I cannot imagine a much worse crime than that of the man you have told me of."

"He burnt down one of the groves at Otaroo."

On saying this, the man reverently lifted his hat, and relapsed into silence. This was the first hint I had of anything like the existence of a religious belief or service among these people, but I could not obtain any further information on the subject at that time.

We had been travelling rapidly, and were now approaching the termination of the plain, in a south-westerly direction from K'ootar. We now halted, and under the shelter of a high rocky peak, which started out of the plain, we dismounted to refresh ourselves. It was about seven o'clock, and as it was our intention to reach a certain posting-house by eleven o'clock, we halted for half an hour only, entering the mountain range at eight o'clock. For the next two days we did nothing but climb steep, dangerous paths, hedged in by yawning precipices on the one side, and blank stone walls on the other. But our little beasts were hardy and sure-footed; never giving a chance in all the journey. Towards the end of the second day we met a company descending the mountain. They were laden with gold, and were strongly armed. After we had passed the descending troop, I asked my companion,—

"Is there ever any attempt to rob these escorts of their gold?"

"There used to be," he replied, with a strange smile.

"And were these attempts successful?" I asked.

"I will answer you presently," was Lanna's reply.

We now entered a plantation of thick trees, through which the road lay. When we reached the centre of this grove I was conscious of an excessively offensive smell, which poisoned the whole atmosphere. Before I could obtain any answer to my eager questions my companion stopped, and, pointing to a tall tree, showed me the corrupting bodies of five men. They were enfolded by the coils of a huge snake, which was wound around them very elaborately. The snake, of the boa-constrictor kind, was about seventeen feet in length. Of course it was dead, and had been used as the instrument of death to the unfortunate men.

"There," said the officer, "there are the men who attempted to rob a guard of Orangwŏks of the gold they were carrying to the king."

He said this with a curl of contempt on his lip.

We were glad to get beyond the range of this poisonous stink. In another hour (we were still rising) we entered a small plain enclosed in the mountains. It was a black, weird-looking spot; no trees grew upon it, and only the most stunted kind of herbage. The sun never shone upon it, for his rays were intercepted by the high mountain peaks that were all around. Only in one place did the light of the sun fall, and there only for half an hour in the day. As we entered this dreary-looking level, our leader, pointing with his sword to a high ledge of rock, considerably beyond us, said,—

"There are robbers. Orangwŏks, ready."

And in a short space six of our troops were careering at full speed towards the robbers, who sat for a time in ignorance of our approach. No sooner, however, did they see us, than they rose to their feet, and began to scramble up the steep hill-side with great speed. Our troop followed them on their ponies, the little things climbing like goats. We watched the pursuit with interest; all except the chief and his immediate friends, who sat apart and took no notice of such contemptible things as robbers. Our interest was sustained by seeing that the troop was gaining upon one of the robbers, who had separated himself from his companions. At last springing up the steep face of a huge rock, he signified by his movements that he had escaped. His triumph was of short duration, for one of the troop, springing from his pony, climbed up the face of the same rock, and, on the robber attempting to push him back again, grappled with him, and pulled him down the steep side of the cliff. We heard one cry, as the two men came rolling down first the rock and then the steep side of the hill, thumping from stone to stone like huge boulders. When their descent was checked they were both dead—bruised and beaten to pieces. After catching the unfortunate trooper's pony, and taking off his dress and arms, we rode on as if nothing had happened, leaving the bodies unburied.

"The king has one enemy less," said my companion, "and one soldier less, but as he has more soldiers than enemies the king is a gainer by this result."

Our chief had hardly condescended to notice the result of the fray, an indifference to human life which did not raise him in my estimation.

CHAPTER XII.

This little episode gave me an insight of the Orangwök character, which was a very unpleasant and painful one. It showed that there was an indifference to human life and suffering, which was surprising, when contrasted with their advancement in some other respects.

We had now reached an altitude of ten or twelve thousand feet, I should think, and began to feel the change in the state of the atmosphere very keenly at night. Next day we continued our advance upward, in a more direct route, and saw at times the line of snow, which was not far from us. I may here say, without particularizing any further, that our route lay through the Tannavorkoo mountains, and that the path which we travelled was cut out of the solid rock in many places, and although well made for a mountain path, yet we had many perilous and difficult passages to pass.

About noon, on the third day, we had

reached the snow limit, and should, my friend informed me, begin to descend at once. No person ever climbed beyond the position we had now attained, for the spirit of Tannavorkoo lived beyond. He could be heard talking to himself frequently, and no one would venture to intrude upon his privacy. It is often said that sailors are superstitious, yet the Orangwöks are as full of superstitions as any sailor that I have ever known. Anything that is unknown to them they invest with life, and strange and terrible powers, and although they do not always worship it, yet they are always afraid of it. They were afraid, I gathered from my companion, of the spirit of the mountain, and gave him a wide berth, by not venturing higher than our present halting-place. We were now fully fifteen thousand feet above the level of the sea.[1]

I had never been so high in the air in my life. The prospect was wonderful and fascinating. The eye was carried over all the lower winter territory of the Orangwöks—the plain which was first entered by the priest and myself. Of course, I could not distinguish any-

---

[1] It must be borne in mind that all the measurements of space and time in this narration are mere approximations to the fact. Trégan had no means of determining either distance or time with accuracy.—ED.

thing at this distance, except the lake, which I formerly mentioned. This I could now see, like an immense blue cloud lying on the ground.

We halted at night, some hundreds of yards lower down than the highest point we had reached at noon. It was well that we had descended so far, for a storm came on during the night, and swept round the mountain peaks with great violence. I had never heard such thunder as rolled about the rocky sides of the range, crash after crash, reminding me of the firing of heavy artillery, followed by a long rolling sound, which shook the hill, coming when least expected, and from unexpected quarters. Roll after roll of thunder, long-continued vivid flashes of lightning, forked, and in broad sheets of flame. Such were some of the phenomena, and these continued for some hours. All the while heavy rain fell, soaking us to the skin, for we were only under the shelter of an old shed made of rough logs, and put up very carelessly. As I listened to the thunder, rolling about so grandly, I could fancy there was some wild spirit upon the mountain—such a fancy had probably suggested itself to the minds of the Orangwöks, and given rise to the superstition of which I have spoken. After the storm passed off, which it did in about two hours, we made ourselves a little comfortable, and waited for the morning.

I was awakened by a loud report, as if of a cannon, followed by noises above our heads. My friend said,—

"Hark! Tannavorkoo speaks. Listen!"

After listening for a short time, I thought I understood the cause of the noises. They reminded me of the breaking up of ice, which I had heard when at sea in southern latitudes, so I concluded that there was a lake above our heads, farther up the mountain, and that it was covered with thick ice, which was now breaking up under the action of the heavy rain.[2]

These sounds, which were frequently heard, were supposed by the Orangwöks to proceed from the spirit of Tannavorkoo, and always portended mischief. This superstition made the old chief, and other members of our party, extremely anxious to descend the mountain; yet no one dared to move until daylight, as the paths were narrow and perilous. By the first streak of light we were on our way down, glad to be on the move, as the cold was intense. Our path was now exceedingly dangerous, as the water rushed over it in torrents, and broke across our road at many

[2] This was probably a glacier.—ED.

points. The noise, too, of cataracts and waterfalls filled the atmosphere with disturbing, although pleasant sounds. In about a couple of hours we were able to travel with greater rapidity, as the road was much better, and from this point all the danger and much of the difficulty of our route were over. We descended with great rapidity. At night the atmosphere was again pleasant, although rather cool. As we lay watching the sky and the large bright stars which filled the field of vision, my companion drew my attention to the flashes of a bright light on our right, and said,—

"Tannavorkoo's kitchen. He is cooking his food."

I looked, and after watching for a time, I saw a deep, rose-coloured light, like that caused by the reflection of a large fire. The light kept changing its outline, rising and falling, and spreading itself about. I could imagine some part of the mountain on fire. There was hanging over the spot a mass of dark clouds, the outline of which was continually changing, being affected by the changes of the light; but the mass itself never seemed to move. As I had seen one volcano in active work, I came to the conclusion that this was a volcano—one of the many in active operation in the interior of the country. It was a grand sight, and I felt a rush of pleasurable feelings as I looked upon these wonders of this unknown land, and felt that I was the first European who had ever penetrated so far. My thoughts naturally went back to my early home, and the experiences of my past life. I recalled the little graveyard, in which lay the dust of my dear father, and wondered would my dust ever mingle with his; and then I reflected upon his teaching, and asked myself how far I had endeavoured to profit by it, and was constrained to confess that I had too often failed. Such thoughts so worked upon my mind, that I rose up from my place, and kneeling down, as my companions slept, offered a prayer to God. I had not done this for years, although I had not lived without the sense of God's presence. My mind was more composed, yet I could not sleep, for I began again to think of the past. I thought of my poor mother, and shed tears at the thought of her sufferings and her sorrow on my account. She would, I felt, never see me again.

Dear Miss Cunningham, to whom I owed so much, rose before me, and I felt compelled to review all her kindness to me; and Philip, my early friend and brother, and our long painful travel, when we ran away from our homes ten years ago—these passed before me. Poor Philip! his bones were lying in the ocean, to wait the coming of the Day of Judgment. And thus my night passed away, in melancholy recollections of the past.

In the morning, I was informed that our journey would terminate on the following day. We were descending rapidly, and entered upon a large valley, filled with trees and rich vegetation. The sides of the mountain were clothed with short trees, of the fir kind in appearance, very much like some of those which grow in our public parks, only much smaller. Here, in the valley mentioned, the trees were large, and the foliage rich and plentiful. I will close this chapter by relating an interesting conversation held between my friend Lanna and myself. On this day, as we rode together, he said to me,—

"I saw you get up last night, and fall down upon your knees; your lips moved. What were you saying?"

"I was praying; speaking to my God."

"Who is he? What is his name?"

"His name is God, and He lives up yonder, beyond Otaroo (the sun)."

At my mentioning the word sun (Otaroo), my companion lifted his hat, and replied,

"Is he, to whom you spoke, greater than Otaroo?"

I replied by suggesting that Otaroo was probably the same God, and that he lived beyond the stars, or beyond the sun (for the Orangwöks think the stars are only little pieces of light stuck in the heavens), and that this name was given to him because it was the only thing worthy to represent him. On my saying this, my companion became thoughtful, and the conversation ceased.

CHAPTER XIII.

The change, when we reached the large valley, was exceedingly agreeable, for the cold farther up the Tannavorkoo had been excessive. We were now warned that travelling was dangerous from other causes, and advised to keep together, and to keep a good look-out. Wild animals were plentiful a little farther down, so too were serpents, for in this part of the country, which was not frequented much by the natives, wild beasts and snakes abounded. By nightfall we had entered upon a broad plain covered with the usual foliage of tropical countries. The heat was now considerable. Next day we should be at the mines.

About eight o'clock the next morning the plain narrowed itself to a large valley, through which our course lay. We halted before entering this comparatively narrow defile, for hills rose on either side of it whose sides were thickly covered with immense trees. Here we were informed that our eyes, those of the prisoners and myself, must be bandaged, as the passage was one of considerable danger. I did not like the idea, and begged that I might be allowed to ride with my eyes uncovered, as I could look upon anything. Lanna, my friend, informed me, however, that it was absolutely necessary that I should be blindfolded, and advised me to submit and leave myself with confidence in his hands, comforting me with the assurance that all would be well. When we had all been bandaged, the guards took hold of our bridles to lead us. I thought the pony's head had been turned about, as we began to move, but was not sure. From a quick ambling pace we passed into a gallop, and I found it very difficult to keep my seat, for I could not assist my judgment with my sight, so I was constrained to hold on by clutching the pony's long mane with both hands. For half an hour at least this pace was kept up, greatly to my inconvenience. At the end of that space of time we halted, and after a few minutes' delay our eyes were unbandaged. We were standing before the mouth of the valley down which we had galloped. We were now informed of the reason for blindfolding us. This was the celebrated serpents' valley, of which one heard so much at Wätárá, and which had much to do with keeping people at the mining country; for it was a dangerous undertaking to travel through this opening, and no other way to K'ootar was known. As we stood here to give our ponies a blow, my guide volunteered to take me back to the entrance of the valley, that I might get a better idea of the way we had come. I consented, and, on our approaching its mouth, I was struck very much by the height and size of the trees. Their clear stems ran up nearly a hundred feet before the limbs began to appear on them, and were very thick. Here too were many palm-trees, whose feather-like plumes gave a graceful appearance to the whole valley. There was also a large tree-flower in this valley, which was now in full bloom. The flower was a bright scarlet, which hung suspended in long folding pendants from the branches. At a distance one might easily imagine these scarlet trees to be trees of fire, whose pendants, as they moved in the wind, were the flames leaping and jumping. I was lost in admiration as I contemplated these things; and as we continued to advance up the valley, new beauties opened out before us.

"Stop! beware, Trégan!" cried my guide in warning tones.

I stopped at once, and, looking forward under his direction, saw a vast snake curled up at the foot of a tall tree in front of us. I could not judge of its length, yet it must have been very great. Another and another of these coils were pointed out by him, and I had an unpleasant sensation of cool perspiration oozing out of the pores of my skin.

"Take care, take care!" he cried out in terror, and catching my pony by the head he pulled me back towards the mouth of the valley.

After we had got away some twenty yards, I saw an immense boa-constrictor curled round the stem of the tree, near which we had been standing. The beast's neck was stretched some ten or twelve feet over the pathway, and its head kept rising and falling in much the same way as I have seen that of a turkey wriggle about. The terrible reptile had evidently been sunning itself, and, having been awakened by our approach, had proceeded to uncoil its immense body in order to obtain its mid-day meal. It was not less than sixty feet long, I am sure, for I counted at least six coils round the body of the tree—allowing seven feet for the length of each coil, and fifteen feet for the head and neck, I made it out about sixty feet long. After this we hurried back to the guard, and reported what we had seen. Several of the prisoners expressing a wish to see the serpent, they were permitted to approach the mouth of the valley to catch a distant glimpse of the boa, with which they were quite satisfied. I learned afterwards—some years afterwards—that this valley was never traversed by any persons; that the escorts really made a considerable *détour*, and came out through a secret channel whose approaches were carefully hidden by trees and rocks. This fact was concealed from the mining population, to hinder their return to K'ootar. They knew of no other path than that through the boa valley, and were too fearful of its horrors to dare an attempt through it. Some had indeed attempted to pass through it, but, as they had never been heard of again, it was universally believed that they had been destroyed by the serpents; and there can be little doubt that such was the case. I have heard somewhere that an army was once stopped by a great snake, and I can readily believe that the boas in this valley would hinder the progress of the bravest army, if not completely obstruct it. From this point our road lay along a well-sheltered plain, the track running by the side of tall, thickly-foliaged trees. In about an hour from our leaving the valley, I was startled by hearing a cry for help, the sound coming, as it seemed to me, from directly over my head. On looking upward I was horrified to see an unfortunate wretch fastened to a tall tree by means of ropes, and near him was a small snake about eight feet long. The snake was standing erect, and hissing at the unfortunate man, who was beating his hands wildly, and trying to avoid the fangs of the serpent.

"Can we not help him?" I asked, greatly excited.

"No, he is a criminal, and must die. Better to die thus than wait to be starved or torn to pieces by birds. He is fortunate."

The snake had now bitten the man, at least so I judged, for he gave a scream of fear and pain, and seized the serpent's head with his half-loosened hands. The venomous beast now curled itself rapidly round the neck and arms of the poor man, and strove to draw its head to the man's face. But desperation gave the poor fellow strength, and for a long time he resisted successfully. At last his strength failed, and we saw, to my great horror, the snake's fangs steadily approaching the man's open mouth, for he was nearly suffocated. I could look no longer, and, turning my head away, continued my journey. Again I remarked that the old chief was indifferent, and gave no more than a single glance at the unfortunate criminal, who was suffering so terrible a death. In another half-mile we saw a number of birds hovering over a tree, and on our reaching it saw another unfortunate creature chained in its upper branches. He was vainly trying to defend himself from the attacks of an immense eagle which sailed backwards and forwards, every now and then descending upon the poor wretch and striking him with its powerful talons. When we were seen the poor fellow cried to us in piteous terms to save him. This, however, was impossible. The old chief was immovable, so we were compelled to ride on, and leave him to his fate. Another and another tree contained the corrupting corpses of men who had shared similar fates. These things made me look upon the governor of the gold-mines with feelings of distrust, and I began to regret that I was so completely in the power of such a cruel despot.

Now we reached a broad river, nearly half a mile wide, formed by the confluence of all the mountain streams. The river was deep and rapid, and sometimes its passage was exceedingly dangerous. It was crossed by means of rough planking laid upon inflated skins, which were kept supplied by proper persons appointed to take care of them. As the planking was not more than three feet wide, and had no protection on either side, the crossing was no pleasant undertaking, especially as the planks jumped up and down under our feet as if they were elastic. They were also deflected by the strong current that was running, so that they formed almost a semicircle whose extreme points were resting on either bank.

Here we all dismounted, and, handing our ponies to the guards, proceeded to walk over the narrow crossing. The ponies, after their bridles had been tied to a long rope, were plunged into the water, one of the guards swimming in front of them, and leading them. They accomplished the crossing with some difficulty, and came safe to the other side.

CHAPTER XIV.

AFTER crossing the river, which is called Irfak, we proceeded in a northerly direction, and arrived in about an hour and a half at the mining country. I had expected to see tents and windlasses, with all the paraphernalia of a digging life, to which I had been accustomed in Australia, and was therefore disappointed to see no such indication at Wătárá, for so was the whole of the gold-bearing region called. For miles the country was covered with men in the dress of the common Orangwŏks, only dirtier, who were engaged in the work of procuring gold. We hardly stopped, but pushed on rapidly until we reached the town of Wătárá. This was the place where most of the miners lived. Here they had their houses, such of them, at least, as possessed houses; here, at any rate, most of them lived. Wătárá, named after the gold-bearing country, was a large town, the largest, indeed, in the kingdom of Orangwŏk. There were fully 10,000 miners living here, and quite 3000 women and children, besides the governor's staff of guards, by which order was duly maintained. Altogether, the population could not be much less than 15,000.

The first night was spent in the governor's quarters, and on the next day, the old chief took me with him on a tour of inspection over the digging country. It is unnecessary to describe this country, farther than by saying that it consisted of hills and valleys, and was evidently formed by some volcanic eruption. The gold was found principally in the valleys, and on the sides of the hills. It was picked out of the surface to a depth of two or three feet. There had been no attempt to sink holes—no attempt to wash the soil. This at once showed me that there was a capital field for the exercise of the knowledge I had gained on the Australian diggings. I remarked this to my companion, who had never opened his lips since we had left his camp, or quarters.

"It will be well for you, if it is as you say. Words should not be like the wind."

This was said in an ominous tone of voice, and did not restore my confidence in the old tyrant. I said no more, but on reaching the quarters of the governor, said,—

"Give me wood and tools, and I will prove my words."

I had resolved to make a "long Tom," such as I had seen in Victoria.

On the hills we had visited, the men were picking out gold nuggets of various sizes—the small gold was entirely lost. I saw that the soil which was thus thrown aside, was full of fine gold-dust, not that I could actually see the gold in the earth, but I knew from my knowledge of gold-digging that such was the case, that where there were such rough pieces there would be plenty of fine gold. Hence my idea of the "long Tom," for I proposed to carry this earth and wash it in the river below, by means of the apparatus I was making. Several rough pieces of wood were brought, by some assistants, placed at my disposal, and, with the help of the flint tools, I succeeded in knocking up a "long Tom" composed of three compartments, and having a fine sieve made of twisted grass or hemp. The old chief came every day to look at my work; so, too, did my young friend, the officer of the troop, and he gave me a hint that the former was by no means too well affected towards me.

"However," he said, "your life is quite safe, for he would not dare to harm you if you are successful in your undertaking, as I am sure you will be."

"And how long must I remain here," I asked, "if I succeed in what I have promised to do?"

"That depends, to some extent, upon the governor. You see he can send what report he likes about you, and if it suits him to keep you here, he may endeavour to do so. Have you any friends in K'ootar?"

"Yes, old Kayhar is my friend." The name of Lamlam was on my lips.

"Well, his influence may be of use to you some day, so do not despair, even if the governor should turn out to be unfavourable to you."

After my "long Tom" was finished, I explained to my young friend how it was intended to act. He understood at once, and took as much interest as myself in proving the success of my scheme. The day following the "long Tom" was carried by half-a-dozen Orangwöks to the river under the hill, where much surface-gold was being obtained. At eight o'clock I informed the governor that all was ready, and begged him to be present. Lanna and several other of the officials also came to watch the proceedings. I had placed the "long Tom" on the bank, under a slight fall of water, which I had diverted by means of a bark trough into the "Tom" itself. I was thus able to keep a steady current running continually through the "Tom." Several skins full of the most likely-looking earth, from a spot which I had seen rich in nuggets, were procured and were thrown into the upper compartment, which was about six feet long, and divided from the lower by a ridge of six or eight inches high. I continued to puddle this earth until all the clay had been washed away, and nothing but sand and stones remained. Another supply of earth was brought and treated in the same way, and still another, until I thought that I had had sufficient to give me a very good chance. I now turned the water off and began to pick out the stones. They were all washed perfectly clean, and as I tossed them out, the governor and my young friend standing close by my side, watching intently every operation, I scanned them carelessly, not expecting to find a nugget in the upper compartment. How great was my surprise and pleasure, therefore, to see a large lump of gold lying among the stones, perfectly bright. I seized it eagerly, and handed it to the old chief, who clutched the valuable mass most greedily. It weighed a pound and a half, I should say.

After this every stone was examined with care before it was thrown away; but no farther discovery was made. This one find, however, excited my highest hopes, and I now proceeded to wash out the fine sand which had collected in the other compartments. As the water carried off every successive coating of sand, and the layer of each compartment became smaller, I could see occasional gleams of gold, which warned me to proceed with greater caution; so I now turned off the water a second time, and drawing the attention of the governor and his officials to my movements, drew out the first plug, and scraped all the glittering sand, which was mixed with good coarse gold, into a stone dish. The old chief bent over the "long Tom" eagerly, as he saw that the sand was only a thin coating lying on a basis of gold. After repeating this process in the other compartments, and scraping from each one a large quantity of fine gold, I took the dish to the river-side, and washed off the sand very carefully, still watched by the eager eyes of all the officials. At last, to my own surprise and delight, I found that I had about two pounds of fine gold remaining in the dish, which I handed to the governor for inspection. He was amazed at the result, and could not trust the evidence of his senses. He required me to wash out some more soil, which I did, he superintending the collection of every skinful of earth, to see that no gold was intentionally mixed with it. Again the same process, and again a similar result, only this time there was no nugget among the stones, and a smaller quantity of gold in the "Tom." I explained to him that the quantity of gold would differ at times, as the yield depended entirely upon the quality of the soil for gold-producing purposes; but that whatever of fine gold the earth contained was collected in the manner that I had shown him. He was satisfied with the result, and was now exceedingly civil to me, asking me to dine with him, which I was glad to do, as it was now noon and I was very hungry.

The old chief kept a good table, as we Europeans would say, and had fowl, fish, yams, and rice laid before me (for he did not dine himself). He gave me also plenty of eu to drink. His present kindness relieved my mind of some of the anxieties which the young officer's words had aroused within me, and towards evening my friend reassured me completely by saying,—

"You are quite safe now. I shall report all that you have done to the king and to your friends. Your services are too valuable to be lost."

In a few weeks Lanna was required to start for K'ootar in charge of a quantity of gold which was ready for transmission, so he came to me to become the bearer of any message I wished to send, and to bid me good-bye. It occurred to me to write a few words to Lamlam, hoping that she might be able to read them, or at least that she might learn to spell them out. After writing a few lines, I asked him to deliver the bamboo in which I had deposited the paper to Lamlam, and bade him good-bye. With a word of warning in my ear he was gone.

CHAPTER XV.

As it is not my intention to give a full account of my digging experience, I shall here say that I remained nearly five monotonous years at Wătárá, and might have been there to this day had it not been for the energy and affection of my friends. The digging life was not by any means a desirable one. The miners spent all they earned in gambling (strange how this vice exists as much among savages as in the midst of the highest civilization!), and lived generally a miserable life, brawling and fighting. The governor, as this tended to the increase of his power, did not discourage this state of things, so that very few of those who came to the mines ever returned again to K'ootar. They could do so, on their obtaining a certain amount of gold, proportioned to the crime which they had committed, but not otherwise. As the men got accustomed to the reckless life of Wătárá, they lost all desire to return, and the great majority spent

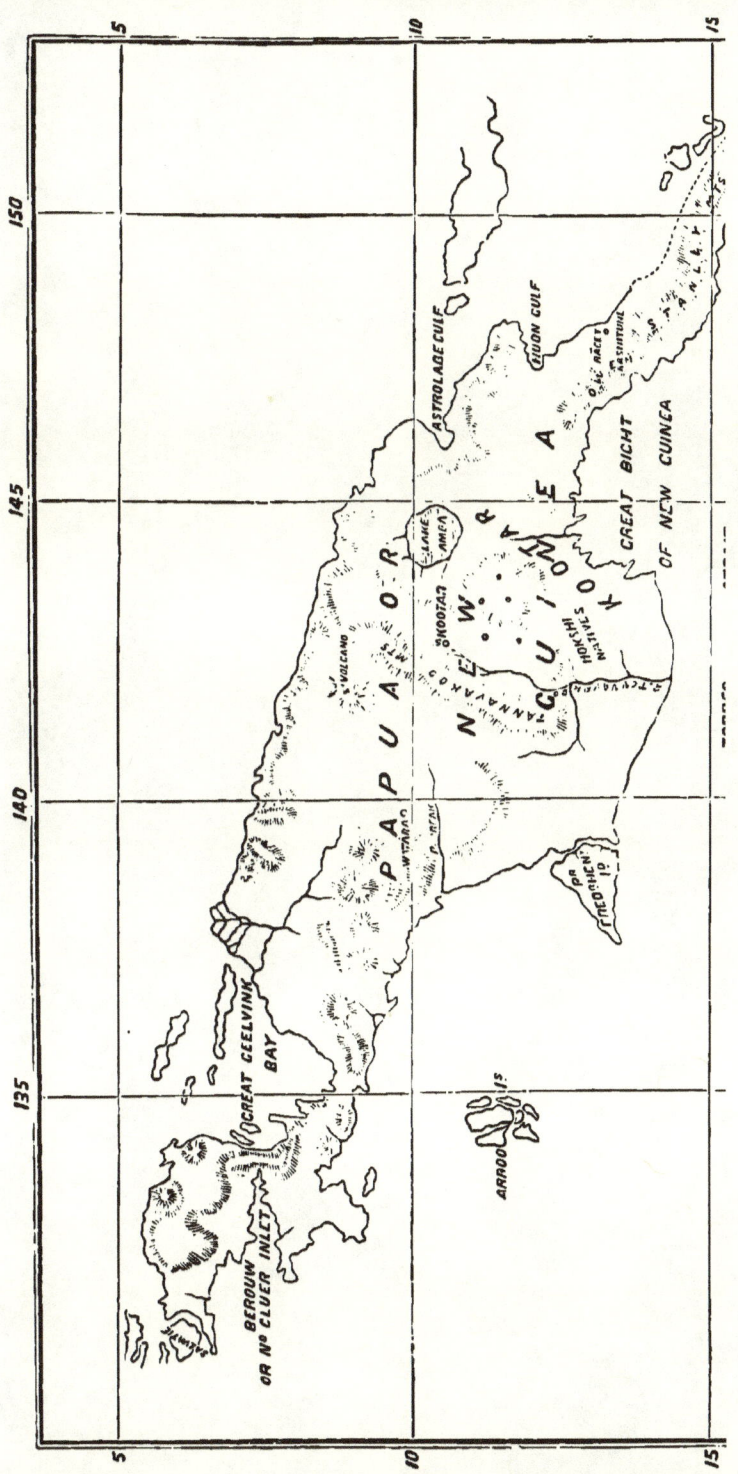

the remainder of their days in this territory. Some of them committed further crimes, viz. hid or stole the king's gold. In this case, if they were convicted, most terrible was the fate which awaited them. They were exposed in trees, sometimes being allowed to starve to death; at others, being regularly fed, and kept alive to be the prey of snakes and birds. If any one attempted to recover his liberty by escaping, he simply lost his life; either he was starved upon the mountain range, or he was destroyed in the terrible valley of the serpents. The monotony of the life at Wätárá was broken occasionally by an overflow of the Irfak, the river that I have mentioned, or by an outbreak of the nearest volcanic mountain. I had an experience of each of these while I was at Wätárá. But to resume, I was at first constantly employed in directing the making of "long Toms" and cradles, as it had been resolved to bring them into general use. Further, I taught the miners to *sink holes*, in order to obtain the precious metal, and I was fortunate enough to be successful in my first shaft. This success improved my position immensely, and brought me into still greater favour with the old chieftain. The country was exceedingly rich in the precious ore. It was found in every direction, and in large quantities. I have picked after a heavy fall of rain, a piece of ...id from the surface weighing, I am certain, fifty pounds. One day I was sitting upon a piece of quartz cropping above the surface; this stone had been used for a resting-place for months; on this occasion I began to beat it with my flint hammer, and a large piece of the reef flew off, exposing a mass of gold embedded in the quartz. Here was a new field for my operations, so, breaking off a large lump of the rock, which was spotted with gold, I took it to the governor, and showed it to him, explaining the difficulty of obtaining the gold from the stone, but asking his permission to try (which was readily granted). I got several pieces of quartz, veined thickly with gold, and tried to break them to small grains. After destroying several flint hammers in my attempts, I found I had made very little progress; so, resolving to try the effects of fire, I put the quartz into a kiln, heated to a great degree of heat, and kept this fire up for several days, as I had known men engaged in burning limestone do. When I found the quartz was pulverized, and the gold melted, I let the fire go out, and I obtained several pounds

of gold from the cold ashes. All this, of
course, took time, yet the life I lived was
monotonous enough, except when it was
varied by a fishing or a hunting expedition,
which was rather frequent, as there were
abundance of fish in the Irfak, and we were
dependent upon the river and the forest for
a large portion of our food supply. Rice
was grown, and yams, and other vegetables
were plentiful, besides such fruits as are
common to tropical climates — cocoa-nuts,
dates, and raisins. The first year of my stay
at Wätárá I had been appointed, by the
governor, overseer of all the mines, and a
part of my duty, in this capacity, was to
receive and account for all gold that was
procured. I was in the habit of keeping
memoranda for my own pleasure of the gold
that was collected from the mines. I mention
this as it was of use to me afterwards.
About the middle of the second year I was
displaced from my position, which was taken
by one of the governor's own creatures, and
I myself was put to employment of a less
responsible character. I understood this
change to mean that I was no longer in the
governor's favour, although how I had
offended him I do not know. At the end of
two years, a little incident occurred which

gave me much pleasure. The officer in command of one of the troops, arriving from K'ootar, brought me a neat head-dress, which had been committed to his care by old Kayhar, the chief. It was to be given into my own hands, he said. I felt that I owed this little attention to Lamlam, and was greatly pleased by it. Another two years passed away, making four years of banishment from K'ootar. I knew now that I was under the displeasure of the governor, yet did not know the reason. During these two latter years, several events occurred to break in upon the dull routine of our life; one was an eruption of the volcano on one of the spurs of Tannavorkoo. For some days before the eruption, the atmosphere was dull and heavy, and towards evening the sky became lurid and dark, blotting out the stars. Soon after we saw the bright flames shoot up to the height of several hundred feet from the crater. This was repeated many times, for several days after which the crater began to discharge its molten flood, which ran for miles over the country, doing a vast amount of injury, and causing the loss of many lives. A great panic fell upon the population of Wätärä, as the lava threatened to reach the town itself. Shortly after this event, the overflow of the Irfak occurred, which threatened to destroy the town. As I have mentioned before, the Irfak is formed by a confluence of many tributary streams, and attains a considerable width almost as soon as it issues from the mountain. It is thus exposed to sudden overflows, some of them of a dangerous nature, for whenever the snow begins to melt, the torrents run down the sides of the great water-shed, and, rushing into the channel of the Irfak, overflow its banks for fully a mile and a half. The river is thus only crossable with safety at certain times. These risings can rarely be anticipated. The one to which I now refer came on after a week's heavy rain, followed by a sudden burst of heat. Some of the experienced miners watched the signs with anxiety, and warned their companions of the danger of an overflow. As we were fully twelve miles from the river, we paid too little attention to these warnings, and went to our beds as usual. In the middle of the night I was awakened by a dull, heavy roar, like the rolling of waves upon a distant shore. As the noise continued, I sat up to listen, and could hear distinctly a loud, roaring noise approaching. Immediately I thought of the warnings which had been uttered about the overflow of the river, and, springing from my bed, ran outside. It was a clear, moonlight night, most fortunately. Others had been aroused, and a large crowd was in the street; some ran backwards and forwards, crying out that the spirit of Tannavorkoo was coming; others stood, like myself, watching the southern approaches to the city. There was no time to escape, for I had heard that a flood travels swifter than a horse could gallop. The governor's troop, however, were ordered out, and directed to escape to the high hills, ten miles beyond Wätárá. All this had occurred in less than fifteen minutes, so at least I should think, for I could not take any note of time under such circumstances. We saw now the long, dark wall of advancing water, coming on with a dull, but deafening roar. Every person escaped to the upper stories of the houses. The highest houses were filled with the poor creatures seeking refuge. When the column of water, which was about six feet high, struck the first row of houses, there was a great crash, and the enemy was upon us, sweeping through the streets, and carrying away everything in its fierce flow. Few lives comparatively were lost; not more than a hundred and fifty persons were drowned, and these would not have been sacrificed if they had not insisted upon trying to save their property from the rushing flood. There had been several previous overflows, but this was the worst that had been ever experienced. It occasioned a great loss of property, and all mining was suspended for a long time. This overflow took place in the third year of my captivity, and, following close upon the eruption of the volcano, quickened my desire to escape.

I have mentioned the fact that we sometimes went upon hunting expeditions. With the account of one such expedition, which was the most strange that I have ever heard of, I will conclude this portion of my adventures in Wätárá.

The governor punished his criminals, as has been noted, by chaining them in high trees, near the valley of the boa-constrictors, leaving them generally to die of starvation and fear, or from the attacks of snakes and eagles. These terrible punishments were of frequent occurrence, for the Orangwŏks have no sense of the value of life, nor have they any sympathy with human suffering. One element in the sufferings of these poor captives, was the fear that the dreaded serpent of the valley would come forth and attack them, winding its terrible coils around the body, and crushing the trembling wretch to death. None had been ever known to leave this valley until the occasion now referred to. Word was brought that an immense boa had escaped from the pass, and had travelled down a distance of ten miles toward Wătárá, drawn, as was supposed, by the presence of the criminals in the trees. Whatever was the cause, here was one of these huge reptiles on the high road, and it might at any time come on to Wătárá itself. So it was resolved to form a hunting party, and attack the beast. Many a brave heart quailed at the idea, but a large party was formed, of which I was one, well armed with spears, swords, and bows and arrows. This forlorn hope was followed by a numerous army of beholders, ready to assist, in the event of the reptile being killed by us, and equally ready to run away in the event of his being victorious. We started from Wătárá about eight o'clock, hoping to arrive at the object of our foray about ten or eleven o'clock, and to catch him taking his midday nap. After crossing the Irfak, we turned into the highway, and proceeded with great caution, for the monster might have already made a nearer approach to the town. In about half an hour we halted, and resolved to send out a couple of scouts. As there was some hesitation about volunteers, I offered to become one, and was accepted.

The reader may be sure that I moved on with great care, scanning narrowly every tree, and examining every bush lest our enemy might lie concealed in it. In another half-hour, we reached a high tree, where criminals were frequently chained. Its limbs, which spread out in all directions, were of a straggling nature. After slightly glancing at its stem, and its branches, we prepared to ride on under the tree; but my little pony beginning to tremble and snort, I warned my companion that there was something near.

"It is the skeletons," he said; "the pony is afraid to pass the bones of men."

There seemed to be reason in this, so I tried to force her gently past the tree. Again she snorted, and ran back, trembling violently. I could not understand this, and looked up again to the tree, to examine it more carefully. As I did so, I met the eyes of the terrible serpent fixed upon me, not more than ten feet above my head. It was approaching me with subtle movements. I thought of the stories I had heard of snakes fascinating those who came within reach of them, and began to feel that I was lost.

My pony too could not move, and the brute's head was swinging itself nearer to me. His neck and head were hanging from a high branch, and looked for all the world like a loose limb hanging from the upper part of the tree, his folds being hidden in the midst of the green leaves.

As the serpent oscillated to and fro, it found that it had not sufficient length of neck to reach either myself or the pony, and began therefore to shake out a reef, as we sailors would say. This action disturbed the leaves, and shook them down in dozens to the ground. My companion, now seeing my condition, came to my help, catching hold of the pony's head, and leading her beyond the snake's influence. I had felt paralyzed, and should, I fear, have perished, had it not been for the assistance of my companion. We now rode back to the troop, and informed them of our discovery. All at once pressed on to attack the monster. On our return he was coiled around the upper limbs of the tree, beyond our reach—an immense brute. The Orangwöks kept at a respectful distance from the enemy, who took no further notice than that of fixing his keen, bright-looking eyes upon us. I confess, after my late experience, I did not care to get into too close quarters. The thing was beyond our reach; what was to be done? We could not watch here until it came down. Could we not get it down by stratagem? This was suggested, on which it was resolved to tie an old pony under the tree, in sight of the boa. I commiserated the fate of the unfortunate pony. Not so the Orangwöks, they had no sympathy with pain or suffering in any form. One of the followers who was at a distance was compelled to dismount, and give up his little horse to the officer in command of the troop. She was then led under the tree and tied to its stem by one of the volunteers.

This being done, we waited with our spears couched. Several of our number had been using their arrows, but without success, as the folds of the reptile were well concealed in the leaves, and those who shot at him were not good marksmen. Presently we saw the beast uncoiling itself, and swinging his head and neck towards the place occupied by the pony, who now began to snort and tremble greatly. After an unsuccessful attempt to reach his victim, the boa still further uncoiled itself, and began to descend. It was now level with the pony's back, the poor creature being paralyzed in every limb with fear.

We waited until it had taken several coils around the pony, and then rushed on. I had dismounted, distrusting, from my previous experience, the little horse I rode. As we all charged in upon the beast, several of those who were mounted were carried on one side beyond the boa, several stopped short, and I found myself alone close upon it. I could see its baleful eyes, and hear its breathing, and felt a most unpleasant sensation. Nevertheless I lifted my spear and drove it through its thick body. Before I had time to make a second attack, the serpent had uncoiled its head, and began to attack me, the pony falling down upon the ground from fright. My sensations are not to be described. I ran back, and found myself rapidly followed by the fearful serpent, and, to make matters worse, the troop made off at full speed, screaming aloud. I gave myself over for lost; but as I had a good start of the reptile, I did not lose heart. There was a small stream (one of the tributaries of the Irfak) directly in my path, about twelve feet wide and four or five feet deep. As the boa was now gaining on me (indeed I might as well try to outrun a zebra), I determined to take to the water. I reached the bank as the quick strokes of the terrible creature seemed at my back. I fancied

I could feel his hot breath upon my neck. I sprang at once into the water, and dived, swimming under the surface some distance. I knew that serpents often swam in the water, and did not therefore expect to escape by merely getting into the stream. The fact is, it was my only chance of escape to dive as I did out of sight.

After I had been down fully a minute, I raised my head, and was conscious of a loud lashing of the water. I saw also the head of an alligator or crocodile. "Out of the frying-pan into the fire," I thought, strangely enough, at such a moment, and made again for the bank, the loud splashing continuing. On my reaching the bank, half expecting to find the boa waiting for me, I was surprised to see nothing of it. On my looking towards the water, which was beaten into foam, I beheld a sight which transfixed me with astonishment. The boa was engaged in deadly conflict with a vast crocodile. Its tail was wound round the stem of a strong tree on the bank, and several of its folds were coiled around the saurian reptile. I half thought of cutting the serpent's tail, yet, after my late experience, decided that it was wiser to leave it alone. I have since found that it would have been a good thing to have cut the tail off, as it would have weakened the serpent considerably. I hastened back to the main road, and when I appeared my companions were astonished to see me come back safe and whole. They crowded round me while I told them how I had escaped, and of the fight between the crocodile and the boa. Again we determined to advance to attack the reptile, but resolved to wait until he had swallowed his victim, after which, it was said, he would sleep. Some of our company were told off to watch, and the rest of us sheltered ourselves from the burning heat of the tropical sun. After he had eaten the crocodile, he coiled himself up to sleep, and while in this condition we attacked him, and I am thankful to say, without loss of life, killed the great brute, and cut off its wrinkled head. The snake measured seventeen yards in length. I do not wish to take part in another such hunt while my life lasts. The remembrance of this one is even now full of painful and unpleasant sensations. We returned to Wätárá with flying colours, and celebrated our victory with the beating of drums. I was the hero of the day, and was held in greater honour by all the Orangwŏks, in consequence of the part I had taken. So ended my boa hunt.

CHAPTER XVI.

In my recontre with the boa-constrictor, described in the last chapter, I had been handled rather roughly, and had my clothes torn; my hat or cap, for it was like the head-dress usually worn by the Orangwöks, had been injured and ripped slightly. On my getting back to my home, I overhauled it for the purpose of repairing. I was unwilling that a memento of my friends should be destroyed. The cap was the one sent to me by Kayhar. As I was examining it I was surprised to see through the rip a piece of paper. Immediately I thrust in my fingers, and pulled out a long sheet of foolscap with writing on it. I now recalled the fact to mind, that I had noticed when I first received the head-dress that it contained some substance within which crackled as I handled it; but I had concluded that something had been put into the hat to stiffen it. I spread out the paper with eager, trembling hands, for I knew it was a communication from Lamlam, and with some difficulty made out the following words, which sent a thrill of delight through me and raised my highest hopes. Of course the communication was not in English, but the following is a fair rendering of the words :—

"Lamlam salutes her friend Trégan. Your words came to me, O my friend! many moons ago, but Lamlam could not hear them, because she was without knowledge. But the friendship" (a better word would, I think, be love) "which she has for Trégan made her hearken diligently" (try to learn), "and now the words of Trégan have spoken to her, and have made her heart glad. O my friend! Lamlam would like to look upon your face. She never forgets the morning that Trégan went to the hills. My father, Kayhar, has been raised to the dignity of the wise men, and sits in the dark room. He is Trégan's friend, and now the king has consented that you, O my friend! shall return to K'ootar. An order from the king to the governor is taken by the troops. In another moon Lamlam will look upon the face of Trégan and will be glad. Farewell!"

Alternate feelings occupied my mind on reading this document. It had been written two years ago, and yet I was at Wătárá, having never heard one word of any order that I was to return to K'ootar. I was constrained to feel that I was in the power of the old tyrant, who was keeping me here for some reasons of his own.

Poor little Lamlam! Two years had she been waiting to look upon my face, and had waited in vain. I was now no nearer to K'ootar than when she wrote. On a careful consideration of all the circumstances of my position, I came to the conclusion that the old chief had some strong motive for wishing to keep me at Wătárá, and that I could only escape by proceeding with great care and caution. He had at his command two thousand soldiers, and could, if he occupied the Monakim passes, make himself entirely free of K'ootar. Whether such was his intention I could not say, yet the thought occurred to me as I deliberated on these circumstances.

If the king had sent an order for my release, and I could not doubt that he had, it seemed very much like an act of rebellion that I was still kept by the old chief in captivity; and I knew that if he felt it to be necessary to his own safety that I should be made away with, he would not hesitate a moment about sacrificing my life. This resolved me to act with the utmost caution. My first step was to write a letter to Lamlam explaining my position, but how was I to send this communication? I had for the last two years been kept out of the way of the escort on one pretence or another, and, moreover, could not ask one of the officers in command to take my communication for me without the old chief's consent, which I felt would not be given. I resorted to the following stratagem :—First, I obtained the governor's consent to my sending a small present to Kayhar in token of my appreciation of his past kindness to me. I then, with great difficulty, divided a gold nugget into two pieces, and, filing out the inside, made room for a short letter, which I then squeezed in, afterwards fastening the two sides of the nugget with a kind of cement. This done, the gold looked as natural as if it had just been washed out of the " long Tom." It was, however, only a matter of time for the cement to dissolve and the pieces to separate, on which my letter would appear. I now rubbed and polished the gold as for an ornament, and, putting it into a piece of bamboo, took it to the governor. After examining it closely, he allowed me, in his presence, to give this to the officer in command of the troop. When the escort had passed out of the town on their return to

K'ootar, I began to breathe more freely, and to hope that my *ruse* would bring me freedom. I determined, however, that I would not depend upon one shot, that I would try again and again.

Thus several months passed, and I heard nothing more from K'ootar; for although I had determined to be on the look-out, yet I was generally out of the way when the escort arrived and departed. After about four months had elapsed I was sent away as usual to a distant part of Wătárá; but feeling sure that some communication would arrive, I resolved to return and visit the escort's quarters. This I did in the night-time. The first person I spoke to was Lanna, my old friend, who was overjoyed to see me. After some mutual inquiries of a personal nature, I explained to him my position, and gave expression to my fear that I had not been treated fairly by the governor. Lanna seemed to feel the gravity of the communication I had made to him, and confirmed my fears by saying that he had also understood that an order for my release had been sent to the governor two years ago; but he had been further told that I had preferred to stay at the gold territory, and as this was a common experience, nobody was surprised at it, although he said some of my friends, especially those who had interested themselves in my favour, were very much grieved at my decision.

I now explained to him that I was acting in disobedience to my instructions in returning to the town, and prayed him not to mention the fact of my visit to his quarters. This he readily promised to do, and also said he would render me any assistance which lay in his power.

"What can be the governor's reasons?" he asked. "Have you offended him?"

"Not in any way that I am aware of."

"The gold-yield has fallen off very much latterly, that may be the reason," he added.

"Fallen off—impossible!" I exclaimed; "it was never so large."

"Trégan, be careful what charges you make," he replied, standing up. "I am your friend and will not, therefore, take any notice of your rash words. Yet, do not repeat them, for it would subject you to a terrible death, to make such a charge as your words imply against a chief."

"Lanna, my friend, I do not care. I repeat, the mines never yielded so much as they have done these last two years. Even the year of the flood the yield was greater than on the previous years. I kept an account of all gold received for some time, and know pretty correctly what was raised out of the earth."

Lanna became very serious and thoughtful at this, and at last, after deliberating for a time said :—

"You say you kept an account of the gold returns for a year. Have you that account? Let me see it."

"It is at my house, but I remember the amount;" and I told him.

He was struck with amazement, and said in a subdued voice, not more than two-thirds of that amount ever reached the king's treasury.

"Trégan, there is something wrong, and I see now the reason of your being kept here. I will deliver you. But do you leave me and return to your post. Come to me again in seven days, and I will advise you what I have resolved upon. We must proceed with caution, for the governor is powerful; yet the king shall not be robbed of his own."

I returned to my post twenty miles beyond Wătárá, and waited anxiously for the week to pass. At the end of that time I again met Lanna at the place appointed, which was outside of the town, lest our movements should be watched. He had decided to take me back to K'ootar on his own authority, "but," he said, "you must yourself join us beyond the Irfak, near the valley of the serpents. I leave Wătărá in two days."

After he had undertaken to obtain my papers for me and my Bible—the only book I had, for I had left the "Pilgrim's Progress" with Lamlam—we separated.

I was now greatly excited, and in high hopes that I should return to K'ootar. I indulged in agreeable visions of the future, and saw myself at one time a great chief in the kingdom of Tannavorkoo; at another, returning to my home laden with wealth and fame.

On the third day I sent my men to another part of Wătărá, directing them to remain there several days, and I myself rode on to the Irfak. I reached it before nightfall; as I had had to make a wide *détour* in order to avoid those engaged in digging operations—even as it was I was seen by several of the miners. After crossing the Irfak I rode quickly to the serpent valley, which I reached before the sun had set, and took a farewell look at the terrible opening. One of the troop was waiting for me according to agreement, the others having gone on through the narrow pass. My guide showed me the concealed entrance, and led the way through it. Lanna and his troop were waiting on the other side, on the large plain of which I spoke in my account of the descent from the mountain. It was resolved to halt here for the night, and to proceed before dawn towards Tannavorkoo. I should not feel at my ease until I had placed the mountain between Wätárá and myself. The cold was intense, and the narrow paths were slippery and dangerous. We, however, passed over to K'ootar without any accident worth noticing. The rotting remains of criminals were still hanging in the high trees by the roadside, and great birds soared about over the revolting spectacle. When we arrived at a certain point in our descent, K'ootar stood out before us, distant about fifty miles. Several other towns could also be seen, and as the weather on the plain was about equal to spring-time in France, we had a very agreeable view of everything. The numerous forests, dotting the vast plateau like so many parks, while here and there, as if between the rifts of clouds, were towns and cultivated land, making an agreeable diversity. We were at this point too far down to see the lake on the lower level. We were glad to reach the plateau, as the cold on Tannavorkoo was very great, and the keen wind swept up its sides, increasing our discomfort considerably.

Next day we should be at K'ootar, and I felt some amount of trepidation and excitement in the thought that I should see Lamlam and Kayhar again after the lapse of so many years. We rose in haste early the next morning, and lost no time before reaching the gates of K'ootar. This we did about three o'clock in the afternoon. A great change was evident. People laughed and talked without restraint, turning and staring at us in good homely style.

What was the meaning of all this?

CHAPTER XVII.

The king had gone to his winter residence in the plain, and many of his nobles or chiefs had gone with him, hence the great change which I had seen in the people's behaviour. They were not under the same constraint as formerly. We rode on through the main street to the treasury, to deposit the gold which we escorted. Lanna then invited me to his home, to remain until further arrangements had been made respecting me. A number of chiefs crowded round us eagerly welcoming me back to K'ootar, and inviting me to stay at their houses. As I had already accepted the invitation of Lanna, I firmly declined all other invitations for the present, and departed with my friend. I was eager to call upon Kayhar, and may as well confess that I was no less eager to look upon the face of Lamlam. In explanation of this, let it be remembered that human sympathy is always dear to man, and especially under such circumstances as those in which I was placed. Besides, Lamlam was not black by any means, she was fairer than any of the Orangwŏks, and they were usually of a dark olive complexion. She was also intelligent, and possessed of such gentle kindness. I owed my liberty to her and her father, and had thought continually of her kindness for the last four or five months. Let those who feel inclined to condemn my feelings towards Lamlam, just place themselves in my position, an outcast from all civilized life, and their judgment will, I am sure, be greatly modified.

So soon as I could do so, I asked my friend's permission to visit Kayhar, and this being granted, hurried with a beating heart towards his house. As I neared its entrance, I looked up eagerly for the signs of Lamlam's presence, for she would be aware by this time that I had returned. I saw none, and felt disappointed. I reached the door and found the matting drawn down firmly, and could obtain no admission. I could not understand this, and was much chagrined. It was a great blow to my hopes and anticipations. I returned to Lanna cast down and heavy at heart. He was absent, but on his return all was explained. The king was on the lower level, and with him were his wise men, the ŭŏŏ, of

whom Kayhar was one. All was explained
now, and I felt my spirits rise again.

Next day, after a consultation with the
principal chief in K'ootar, who compared my
account of the gold received by me during
the first year of my residence at Wătárá with
the amount received at the king's treasury,
it was resolved that I should be sent on to the
king and his wise men for examination. The
matter was very serious, as the deficiency on
that year was fully a third of the amount
of the gold actually raised. I was nothing
loth at this decision, and expressed my
willingness to depart at once. On the second
day, early in the morning, we entered the
great plain, and found the atmosphere most
pleasant and agreeable; for although it was
now mid-winter, yet on the lower country
the cold was like the warm spring weather
which one experiences in Australia or the
south of France. The king's palace, for his
house might be called by such a name, was
in a beautiful situation, and was surrounded
by houses for his wise men, and guard-houses
for his troops. The lake was distant about
two miles, and was covered, at this season,
with elegantly-shaped canoes, ornamented at
the stern and stem with ivory and gold,
elaborately worked and surmounted by gor-

geously-coloured feathers. To witness the movement of a fleet of these canoes is a very pleasing sight, and charms one with a sense of elegance and refinement which one does not expect to find so far from European civilization.

While the officer who had accompanied Lanna and myself went to make his report, I was, under Lanna's guidance, able to visit Kayhar's house. We had no difficulty in finding it, and I approached it with such feelings as I had before experienced.

Kayhar was at home, and was about to leave for a consultation with the wise men. He had just been summoned to a council. He was affected to tears when he saw me, and took me by the hand, English fashion, to welcome me. Lamlam had received my present and had discovered the letter. She had not been well, but was now looking better, and would rejoice to look upon me again. At present she was at the lake. "Our ŭŏŏ will not break up until the sun is down, Trégan can then come to me," and the old chief left us. Lanna and I resolved to walk to the lake side, to see the Orangwŏks in their canoes. I, however, had another reason. On our reaching the shore we sat down upon a rock overlooking the inland sea, and looked over its surface, which was dotted with many large canoes moving about gracefully, like so many vast swans. Lanna here began to rally me about the old chief's daughter, and said, "You will have to adopt our customs if you take her for a wife."

"What customs, my friend?"

"You must become brown like us," pointing to his own dark skin, "and dress like an Orangwŏk."

I had never given up wearing my sailor's "ducks," but had on the last remaining pair, which were in a dilapidated condition.

"I shall have to do so directly," I replied, smiling, "for I have no more European clothes to wear. What other customs must I adopt?"

"You must worship Otaroo," he added, lowering his voice and turning his face from the sun.

"That I could not do," I said, "I am a Christian, and worship the God who made the sun."

"Explain to me, my friend, for I have often thought of your words on the Tannavorkoo."

So I endeavoured to explain as well as I could, promising to read to him from my book if he would allow me. I was a little

depressed by this conversation with Lanna, although I hardly knew why. As we rose up from our seats a canoe glided in to the shore, and my friend, catching my arm, said,—
"Hush, there is Lamlam."

My heart sent all its blood to my face as I looked and saw the graceful form of Lamlam springing from the canoe. She was followed by her mother and several other women. I did not care to go forward to speak to them, for I felt all power passing from my body, and in spite of my friend's lively sallies, as I had not been seen, I moved away, and began to return to the palace. I knew that at least in an hour or so I should see my friends, and speak to them. I went back to Kayhar's, and remained waiting for his return. As I sat meditating about the strange events and changes in my life, and thinking fondly of Lamlam, the matting entrance was drawn aside, and she entered the room. On seeing me her colour, yes, her colour changed, and she turned back, only for an instant, however, as in the next moment she rushed forward, and I received her into my arms, kissing her repeatedly. "Oh! Trégan, my friend, my heart is glad, welcome back to Lamlam!"

I confess I never felt so happy in all my

life. A new and indescribable sensation came over me. We had much to say to each other. I found that she had patiently devoted herself to study the letters and words I had written out for her, and that on receiving my first letter she had begun to learn how to combine the letters whose sounds I had taught her. It was wonderful to me that she had been able to pick it all up so quickly, for I remember that when I had received some lessons in shorthand, it had taken me many weeks to learn the signs and their sounds, leaving out their various combinations.

On Kayhar's return, I was informed that the next morning I was to be presented to the king, and was further to tell my story.

So next day I was presented, if such a term can describe my attitude before a savage king or chief, for I lay on my stomach before him, while he, through his chiefs, questioned me about Wätárá and its gold-mines. When I told him of the vast quantities of gold and how it was washed out of the soil, there was a subdued murmur of amazement from all the chiefs and their wives, who were present. Astonishment and indignation filled the breasts of all, the king included, when my story was concluded. It was evident that the governor was a traitor and a rebel, that he had been plundering the king's treasury, and it was resolved at the meeting of the ŭŏŏ that he should be punished by being suspended on a tree. One old experienced warrior advised that a troop of horse should be despatched at once to hold the mountain passes. This sage advice was overruled, as it was now mid-winter. It was therefore resolved that any undertaking should be delayed until the winter was over, and that the fact of my return to K'ootar should be carefully concealed. Directions to this effect were given, and I was authorized to remain at the winter palace until the expedition was ready to start. In the meantime I had determined to ask Kayhar's consent to my marrying Lamlam, who I was sure would not withhold her own. The old chief expressed his pleasure and happiness, but said that it would be necessary for me to adopt the customs of the Orangwŏks, and that on my doing so, leave could be obtained from the king for me to reside in K'ootar. Without further delay I may state at once that at a council of the wise men it was decided that I should, on adopting the customs of the Orangwŏks, be raised to the position of a chief of the third degree, after which I should be permitted to marry a daughter of one of the chiefs; but the whole ceremony was to be deferred until the expedition against the Governor of Wătárá was terminated, for I was to take part in it. I was now anxious that there should be no further delay, and was glad when the time came for the king's return to the upper plateau. This was the signal for the march of the troops, who had been placed under the command of the old warrior formerly mentioned, with Lanna and myself as lieutenants. It was well known that the governor would offer a considerable resistance, as he had now boldly thrown off his allegiance to K'ootar, and stopped the supply of gold.

Before starting scouts had been sent forward to keep our way clear, and some of these now returned with the alarming intelligence that the mountain passes were occupied by the rebels, and that it would be impossible for us to cross to Wătárá. Every one, now that it was too late to take advantage of it, acknowledged the wisdom of the old warrior's advice. We were outmanœuvred by the old rebel, and our case seemed desperate, for no other approach to Wătárá was known. Out of this difficulty I was able to deliver them.

CHAPTER XVIII.

The occupation of the mountain passes by an enemy had never been anticipated by the Orangwŏks. They were now completely perplexed by the fact that the gate to Wătárá was closed, as one of the chiefs expressed it, and there was no other known route, for the range of Tannavorkoo stretched out towards the south until its heights were lost in the far distance. I was, however, satisfied that there was a passage round the southern base of the mountain, and begged permission to seek for a new road to Wătárá. This permission was granted, and Lanna and myself, accompanied by twelve hardy soldiers, started at once in a southerly direction. This afforded me an opportunity of seeing the lower country and of examining the nature of the animals with which it abounded. At the end of six days' travel over the plateau skirting the mountain we came to the foot of the Tannavorkoo, and descended into the plain below, as the sides of the mountain itself were too steep to allow us to attempt their ascent equipped as we were. We had no sooner descended into the valley than we found we were trespassing on the territory of another tribe. So we halted, and after a consultation between Lanna and myself we determined to retrace our steps until dark, and then, in the secrecy of the night, to attempt to pass through the territory of the tribe, which did not appear to be numerous. This we did, and passed in the dark in safety beyond the tribe's confines. In half a day we reached a wide, deep river running in a southerly direction, which I named the Tannavorkoo. As the volume of water was very great, I knew it was no use following the course of the river down to find a shallow ford, so I resolved to plunge in and swim over. This was a dangerous proceeding, and my companions hesitated. I had read of soldiers swimming broad rapid rivers, and had heard it said that there was no danger if you could give the horse its freedom; so plunging into the water I slipped off the back of the pony and got it by the tail, leaving it otherwise free. The little thing swam capitally, and reached the other side in safety. My companions were encouraged to follow my example, and all came safe to land. We had rounded the southern point of the great mountain range! I pointed out with my sword the way to Wătárá, not more than six days' journey from us; and we decided to continue our survey of the country. On the third day we sighted one of the well-known peaks of the range—the Volcano. I drew Lanna's attention to this landmark, and he agreed with me that it was unnecessary to push our examination further; so we began to return, and on the sixteenth day of our leaving K'ootar we re-entered its gates, carrying the glad tidings that a passage had been discovered to Wătárá. A consultation of the ŭŏŭ was held, and it was concluded to despatch an army without loss of time by the route which had been opened up by Lanna and myself. This army was in command of the old warrior mentioned before, but Lanna and myself were to be advanced to the responsibility of chiefs, and share in his command. Our course lay over the same country which we had travelled three weeks before. It was filled with herds of game. Elk, antelopes, buffaloes, bison, tigers abounded. There were also numbers of kangaroo, an Australian animal, called by Orangwŏks "dop-dop." On my pointing these out to Lanna, and explaining that I had seen them before, he replied,—

"I will show you something that you have not seen."

And taking me to a thickly-foliaged tree, he showed me the same kind of animal, only smaller, in a bough of the tree. They were kangaroo, and were feeding upon the leaves. They seemed perfectly at home in the tree, and climbed it with as much ease as opossums. I saw many of the same kind afterwards. The wankoo too were very numerous as we advanced over the plateau.

We had plenty of sport, and kept ourselves well supplied in meat. Indeed we depended upon our hunting to supply food for our small army—about two thousand men. This fact, of course, reveals a weak point in the Orangwŏks' mode of warfare; yet it must be remembered that such an expedition as we were undertaking was altogether unknown to them. It was beyond all their previous experience, and they knew not how to cope with its difficulties. Nature, however, was good to us, and kept us in food. We never wanted for a meal. On the seventh day we came to the borders of the plateau, and were in sight of the camp or village of the savage tribe. Our coming had not been unknown to them, for we were a large host, and they were determined to give us battle. We halted before descending to the lower level, and endeavoured to treat with them.

Our attempts were unsuccessful, a flight of arrows warning us that we must be careful in approaching them. We spent the night upon the high level, and prepared for battle. A council of war, held between the three of us, decided that it would be wise to descend to the lower plain before sunrise, and not to make the attempt in the face of a determined enemy ready to dispute our passage. So at three o'clock we began our march downward, the stars our only light. The hill side was very steep, sometimes almost precipitous; and many a tumble occurred on our passage down. By five o'clock we were on the lower level, drawn up ready to charge our enemies. They were taken by surprise at our unexpected appearance below; nevertheless, they came on to attack us.

Forming into three divisions we awaited the first discharge of arrows, feeling sure that they would pass over our heads. We were not deceived. With a great shout the savages twirled their spears and came on. When within a hundred yards they shot their arrows at us, but did no harm, nearly the whole of them passing over our heads. No sooner had they shot their arrows at us than we charged them with full speed, riding in among the compact mass of negroes, with our spears couched. But for a time they resisted with great bravery, considering the advantages we had over them. In less than half an hour they were put to flight, leaving nearly fifty men dead upon the field of battle, and a large number of wounded. Several of our men were killed and a good many injured. I escaped without hurt, although an arrow entered my bamboo headdress, and remained there until the battle was concluded. During the conflict a great savage endeavoured to wrench my spear from my hand, but I was as strong as himself, and so successfully held my own against him. He would have got the better of me had I not sprung off my pony, which was a very easy thing for me to do, for my feet were already nearly on the ground. On reaching the earth I drew my sword with my right hand, while holding the spear with my left, and made a lunge at my antagonist. He nimbly avoided the blow, twisting the spear round so as to receive the full force of the blow. The spear was shivered to pieces, and the wily negro seized upon the barbed end to use it against myself. I now found that he was a match for me, for he made at me with great fury. I had, however, been taught the use of the foils, and could handle my sword as a Frenchman ought to do; so that, in the end, cool skill prevailed, and I had the satisfaction of seeing my terrible black enemy lying at my feet in the dust.

Our victory was followed by a visit from a chief of the Hokshi tribe, who came for the purpose of concluding a peace, and of granting us a passage through the tribe's land to the Tannavorkoo river. This was a very acceptable result, for we did not wish to fight our way to Wătárá.

After coming to an understanding with the Hokshi chieftain, we accepted his invitation to remain for the rest of the day with his tribe to witness some of the tribal manœuvres. It was strange to think how soon our deadliest enemies, who had been doing their best to destroy us, had in half an hour become our warm friends, and were doing their best to amuse us. As the usages of civilized warfare[1] were unknown among these savages we did not relax any of our vigilance, while we remained among the Hokshi on friendly terms.

[1] Is there such a thing?—ED.

The next day, as soon as the sun had risen, we began our march towards the river, accompanied by several of the Hokshi chiefs, as we felt more certain that the tribe would not attempt to attack us or intercept us as we marched through the wooded plain, while their chiefs were hostages in our hands. Before reaching the Tannavorkoo river, however, we dismissed our newly-found friends, and continued our march alone. On reaching the river banks, where the depth and width of the water were apparent to the Orangwöks, there was considerable trouble in getting them to attempt the crossing. Lanna and myself plunged in, followed by several of the troop which had accompanied us previously. Others followed, until nearly one-half had crossed. The remainder hesitated, and at one time I was fearful that we should leave a portion of our little squadron behind us. Before the day closed, however, the whole of the troop had crossed. The difficulty of such a passage warned us that we must lose no time in pushing on to the Irfak, lest by our delay the rebel governor should draw up his army to oppose our passage over that river; we therefore made forced marches, our hardy little beasts holding out capitally. I do not know what

European ponies to compare with them; they are so hardy, sure-footed, and fleet. By this means, we were able to reach the Irfak on the afternoon of the fourth day. Finding the passage clear, we resolved at once to cross over, and did so. At night-fall we were within fifteen miles of Wătárá. During the night we despatched a trooper to the town to reconnoitre. He returned before day-break, reporting that there were no evidences of any preparation to meet us. We were overjoyed at our good luck. It was as I expected; as the mountain passes were well guarded, the old rebel, not expecting our approach from any other side, had made no preparation to resist an attack. We marched as soon as our scout returned, and before nine o'clock we were at the gates of Wătárá. A hasty defence was thrown up by the rebels, who were not able to concentrate their forces. As few of the citizens had any sympathy with the old tyrant's rebellious movement, we received some assistance from them. But the best help they rendered us was by keeping out of the way, while we charged down the narrow streets, following the retreating enemy. At every point we were successful, for our foes lost heart at the very outset. They had been completely surprised, and thought we must have crossed the heights; they supposed, therefore, that reinforcements would immediately follow us; that we had the whole strength of the kingdom at our back. When the governor fell into our hands, the struggle at once came to an end.

The affair can only be described as a skirmish, and only a few lives were lost, although many more were wounded. In less than an hour after our entrance of Wătărá the rebellion had collapsed. Had it been skilfully conducted, no power possessed by the king of K'ootar could have extinguished it, and a new and rich kingdom might have been constituted on the western side of the Tannavorkoo.

The old rebel was forwarded at once to K'ootar over the mountain passes, which were opened to us, the rebel soldiers surrendering. He was taken before the ŭŏŏ, and having been condemned, was chained to one of the tall trees used for the purpose of execution. Here he died a lingering and fearful death, thus tasting something of the sufferings which had been endured by many others at his instance.

CHAPTER XIX.

I LOST no time in returning to K'ootar, bidding, as it has proved, farewell to Wätárá for ever. I mentioned in a previous part of this narrative, that it had been resolved that I should, on adopting the customs of the Orangwöks, be raised to the dignity of a chief (of the third order), and allowed to marry a chief's daughter. In taking the latter step, I do not wish to be misunderstood. It may to Christians seem a singular thing for a Christian man to marry a heathen woman, of a different colour, and to resolve to live among heathen people instead of trying to return to civilization. Yet it must be remembered that I had given up any hope of ever escaping from the captivity in which I was held; and further, that habit accustoms one to everything. I had become, after more than five years' life among the Orangwöks, accustomed to their ways, and had moreover found them intelligent, and, in their way civilized people. But, above all, what resigned me to stay among them, was the fact of my having conceived a real affection for Kayhar's daughter. After-events will prove that she was in every way worthy of the love of one like myself; that she possessed many qualities which would have been highly esteemed even among Europeans. All this will appear as my narrative proceeds. These circumstances being duly considered, will, I trust, procure a favourable judgment on the step I was about to take; it must be understood, moreover, that I did not renounce my religion as a Christian. I had too often failed to act up to my duty as a professing Christian, yet I never for a moment intended to relinquish that faith. On my return to K'ootar, my proposed marriage with Lamlam was formally sanctioned by the ŭŏŏ, to whom the intention had to be submitted for their approval. First, however, I had to be received among the Orangwŏks, to have my skin stained the same colour as theirs, and to adopt their costume. A house of three stories had been built for me while I was absent in Wătárá, so that there was now no occasion for further delay on any account. The ceremony was, therefore, directed to proceed. I was summoned to the priest's house and required to reside with him for one week.

Here, my skin was stained with some juices until it attained a dark colour, successive coatings having been put upon me by the priest's own hand. This process having been completed, I was clothed in a long but filthy robe, which completely covered me from head to foot, only leaving an opening for my eyes. The priest now put on himself a rich dress covered with ornaments of gold, and directed me to be taken by some of the assisting priests, clothed similarly, only not so gorgeously, to a stream which ran near the sacred grove. Hither I was brought, disguised in the filthy robe that I have mentioned. A large crowd of people were gathered about the banks of the stream, consisting of both men and women. Drums were beaten, accompanied by such other musical instruments as the people possessed. When the priest arrived, he, standing by my side, delivered an harangue to the people, concluding with an address to the sun (or Otaroo), on which all the Orangwöks prostrated themselves, and repeating the name in subdued tones whenever the priest mentioned it in his address. This was the first instance of a religious service which I had witnessed among the Orangwöks. Such services were more common among the Kakshi, as they were more superstitious. Private religious acts there were none among either tribe. Whatever of such services they had were of a public nature, and were always connected with something which affected the public mind. At Wătárá there was no priest, and therefore no religious service of any kind. But to proceed, when the priest's address was concluded—he looked a very striking figure in his bright dress flashing in the sun, and standing with his hands outspread before the crowd prostrate before him. When he had concluded, two assisting priests descended into the water, and stationed themselves ready to receive me. The priest, taking me by the hand, led me to the stream, and, chanting a hymn to Otaroo, whose chorus was taken up by the people, he cast me into the water as the chorus was being sung. I was at once seized by the two priests, and dipped several times under its surface. At each successive immersion the chorus was repeated in louder strains. On the last occasion I was kept entirely under water until my filthy robe was removed. I was then allowed to emerge from my bath— my skin as black as that of any of theirs. When this was seen a loud shout was raised, and Otaroo was invocated, all falling flat upon their faces at the mention of his dreaded name. On my appearing before them, perfectly naked, the priest again chanted a hymn; again the crowd, as before, taking up the chorus. While this was being sung, another priest came forward, and clothed me with the usual dress of a chief of the third class—a kind of smock of fine hemp, beautifully barred with gold. I was now an Orang-wŏk, and hardly knew myself, chiefs and their wives coming forward to congratulate me on having become one of themselves. So ended the performances of that day. Next day I was presented to the king, and received from him a chief's sword. I could now marry Lamlam, and begged her father that there might be no further delay. The usages of the country, however, interfered again, and hindered the performance of the marriage for another fortnight, as no one was allowed to marry until the moon was full. One of these usages was, that whenever a chief's daughter was married a slave was sacrificed, sometimes two or three, or even six—according to the rank of the chieftain—were sacrificed. I did not become acquainted with this barbarous custom until I was requested to lay my hand upon the poor wretch's head in order that the priest might offer him up.

When acquainted with the fact I refused to consent to the sacrifice, or take any part whatever in it. I interceded, moreover, for the man's life to be spared. This could not be, it was said—that if I did not comply with the law or custom, Lamlam must do so. The poor wretch stood by trembling while I expostulated with the priest and Kayhar. This made me the more determined that he should not be slain, so I resorted to a stratagem, for which I hope the reader will not judge me too severely. It was this: I professed the greatest abhorrence (which I really felt) at the intended murder, and declared that if *white* men joined in killing a slave they were hung by the gods upon trees and left to rot. This statement made an impression upon Kayhar, and through him upon the priest. I offered to bring my book in proof of what I said; and, on being requested to do so, I brought the Bible and read the words from Genesis, " Whoso sheddeth man's blood by man shall his blood be shed," altering them to this effect in translating them into Orangwök, " Whoso sheddeth slave's blood the gods shall hang him on a tree to rot." Whether I was justified in doing this, I leave my readers to judge. The course I took had due effect. The man was reprieved, and ultimately his life was spared, on the understanding that he was to be my slave for ever, ready at any time to be sacrificed. On these terms the custom was in my case dispensed with, and our marriage was allowed to proceed. The form of marriage was singular and elaborate.

I proceeded to the sacred grove over night, and was placed in a kind of box or ark, carefully covered in. Before the sun rose, or as soon as his first beams fell upon the grove, which was situated on high ground outside of the city, the priest began to chant certain words intended as prayers, which he continued until the beating of drums announced that the bride was approaching. When she entered the grove, led by the priest and followed by her father and friends, she was taken first to the marble altar on which the poor slave was to have been slain, and then some words were chanted over her head as she lay upon the sacred earth. She was now (on standing up) led round the grove accompanied by her maidens, seeking her husband. Of course he could not be found, being carefully concealed in the chest which I have mentioned, and which she was not permitted to approach. At last she returned to the altar, and there, declaring that she could not find

Trégan, prayed the help of Otaroo. On this the priest demanded gold for the sacred services. On the gold being placed upon the altar, the chanting was renewed, and as the chorus was raised—all as usual joining in it— Lamlam was led towards the chest in which I was hidden. Again the chant was sung, and again the chorus was taken up by the spectators. On this being repeated the third time, Lamlam was introduced into the chest and became my wife. The proceedings having reached this point, the noise from drums, fifes, lars, and voices became deafening, in the midst of which we felt the chest lifted and borne through the air. This continued for half an hour, when suddenly all the noise ceased. We had reached the gates of K'ootar, and were entering its streets. Noise now would have been unseemly. The crowd, however, continued to follow until our bearers stopped, but only for a moment, in the next they proceeded, although with evident difficulty, the chest tilting as if it was being lifted upward. We now felt that the chest was laid upon a floor, and presently all was silent. The sound of footsteps being heard receding in the distance, Lamlam now whispering that we were at home, I opened the side of our carriage and found that we were in our own house on the third floor. We were at home; Lamlam was my wife.

For a whole week neither of us stirred out of our house. It would have been a serious breach of etiquette had we done so, but at the end of that time we were saluted by a horrible din of instruments beating discordantly, which continued for an hour. This was to signify that we were to return to the world, and begin our round of feasting and merriment, with which the marriage of a chief's daughter always concludes. I was glad when it was all over.

CHAPTER XX.

Wannoota, the principal priest, was a man of great intelligence, with a wider extent of knowledge than was possessed by the ordinary chiefs. He was shrewd and far-seeing; ready to perceive the bearing of anything upon his interests. After my marriage he sought me out and became, as I concluded, my friend. He expressed the highest admiration of my ability to talk to a piece of paper or leaf which had marks upon it, and begged me to give him some assistance that he might be able to converse with the "white leaf." I consented to do so, and after giving him a few lessons in the same way that I had given them years before to Lamlam, he made great progress, and evidently grasped the full meaning of our system of writing. After this he visited me assiduously, and obtained from me all the knowledge I could communicate in this way. He also sought eagerly for information respecting the countries of the white men and their religion. To all that I could tell him he listened intently, only interrupting to ask some question, which showed how well he understood the bearing of my remarks.

"Do you not keep your God in your temples?" (or groves.)

"No, our God is in heaven, beyond the stars or beyond the sun."

"There is nothing beyond the sun; nothing could remain up there. How would it hold on? Where, therefore, could your God live?"

"He lives out of sight; no one can see the palace where He resides."

"How do you know that unless you have been there?"

"Our leaves (books) tell us this."

"But did your leaves come down from heaven, and who brought them? Were they thrown down in a thunder-storm?"

To this I answered by explaining as best I could; when Wannoota returned again to his first thought.

"Then, if your God is not kept in His temples, how do the people make offerings of gold to Him? How do they offer sacrifice to Him? And if they do not, how can His priests live and become rich, dressing like the great chiefs of the kingdom? If we only worshipped Otaroo with words his priests would die, and the people would not fear him."

I had been trying to explain the nature of Christian worship to him. I cannot relate one hundredth part of the priest's conversation with me; nor did I at the time see the drift of his inquiries. He professed to be anxious to understand what was in the book from which I had read before I was married. I promised to teach him. The priest and myself were thus thrown a great deal together, and, as he was a well-informed and intelligent man, I gained a large amount of information about the resources of the kingdom of K'ootar—the manners and customs of the people—the distant tribes inhabiting the coast country to the north of the Tannavorkoo. He told me that there were among these barbarian tribes,—tribes of women who lived entirely by themselves, and killed any man who fell into their hands except at certain seasons of the year. That there was another race, called the Kik-Kiks, who had an evil spirit living in the heads of the individual members of the tribe. I could not understand this till afterwards. But I will relate what the priest told me.

"Many years ago," he said, "there was a

great chief, who was very brave and very cruel. In a battle with one of the many other savage tribes, he was struck to the ground by a spear wound which passed through his mouth. As the blow did not kill him he was nursed carefully until he recovered, but when he had recovered it was found that an evil spirit had taken possession of him, and was living in his head. It could be heard talking. Every one felt he was haunted, and avoided him. After a time, his life becoming a burden to him, he departed from the kingdom, and, taking with him many wives, he established a new tribe."

This was many years ago, before Wannoota's three fathers were born. The new tribe thus formed were the Kik-Kiks.

"Another people," he said, "had tails, at least the men had, and whenever they sat down had to make holes in which to coil their tails, for they were very long."

I did not, of course, believe these stories, yet felt there might be some amount of truth in them. Before I left K'ootar I had a slight confirmation of one of these stories. There came a deputation from a distant tribe living in the north, bringing with them a slave which they had captured on their route. As he was said to belong to the Kik-Kiks, I, remembering the priest's tale, went to see the slave. He was an ugly, malformed-looking creature, very forbidding in his appearance. When I drew near to him I could hear distinctly a noise whenever he drew his breath, like the ticking of a clock. I could not believe my ears; yet, there it was. I examined the man, thinking the noise might be caused by some abnormal state of his throat. Yet I could detect nothing unusual. The man was breathing naturally, not in the least surprised at himself, but surprised to find that we did not occasion a similar noise when we drew our breath. Whether there are others like this man I cannot say. It is possible that one or two instances like this may have given rise to the story of a tribe of Kik-Kiks.

My life with Lamlam was a very happy one. She endeavoured in all things to carry out my wishes, even in regard to her dress. Of course I was too much imbued with European customs to be pleased with the indecent costume of heathenism, and I persuaded my wife to adopt a more becoming dress in respect of length than was usually worn. As no one could attend a *levée* of the king's except in the dress prescribed, I thought it better that Lamlam should keep away, giving out that she was not well—as indeed she was not.

We had many pleasant and interesting conversations, which I now hold in affectionate recollection. Although I do not care to reveal the purport of these, yet, to give the reader an insight of her character and mind, I will relate one conversation which we had together soon after our marriage.

(I may mention here that I had not felt satisfied with my marriage until I had read the marriage-service from the Prayer Book, which was bound with my Bible, with Lamlam, and had gone through the ceremonies there prescribed.)

It was after this that the conversation referred to took place.

"How long," said she, placing her hand in mine and laying her head on my shoulder, "did you say you would love me?"

"For ever—until death parts us."

"And won't you love me afterwards?"

"Yes, Lamlam, I will love you in heaven."

"What shall I be like after I die? Shall I be a Wankoo or Dop-dop?"

"No, you will be an angel; better than you are now, and as white as the snow on Tannavorkoo."

She shrank from the idea of becoming white, but she said,—

"Where shall I live then? In what country?"

"In heaven, beyond the sun."

"But there is no place beyond—farther off than Otaroo."

"Yes, there is, Lamlam, but we can't see it."

"Well, but Trégan, how can we get up to heaven? What road shall we go?"

"Oh, we shall have wings, and fly up like the angels."[1]

This satisfied my wife's mind for a time. And we often renewed our consideration of the same subject, as much to my own instruction as to hers, for I found that I was really very ignorant when I came to teach others. And so a pleasant year passed away, a year in which I enjoyed as much real happiness as I can expect to have this side of the grave.

[1] Tregan's idea of angels is a very primitive one. The Scriptures do not say that they have wings.—ED.

CHAPTER XXI.

My happiness was increased at the end of twelve months by the birth of a little boy. It was a strange sensation to me when I first heard the child's cry, as he lay in his mother's arms. I did not feel immediately any special affection for him. I looked upon him as a curiosity, and felt towards him very much as I have felt towards a little puppy. Do not misunderstand me. He was a pretty enough little fellow, with an olive-coloured skin, and large, gentle-looking dark eyes, which wandered all over my face, as I stood watching the little thing as he lay nestling into his mother. He was pretty, and quite as interesting as any other baby ever was. Yet I did not feel that strong paternal love for him which I expected to feel. I liked to stroke him, and would have liked to handle him, only I was fearful of hurting him. However, as time passed, I found all a father's love come, and then the happiness of our household reached its height. As soon as my wife began to get strong, and was able to be about the house, she had congratulatory visits to receive. These were very wearisome, as indeed all the etiquette of these people was, at least to me. But then I had never been accustomed to what is called etiquette, having been all my life a free and careless sailor.

There was now to be a great confabulation among the women of the place, for the purpose of naming the new comer. I was not supposed to be interested in this matter, so I was not taken into the council. This was purely a subject for the women-friends of Lamlam to determine. And so the child was handed about from one to another, every one examining him with care, and commenting upon his various features. All were much surprised to find that he was nearly white. As I was now well stained, and as brown as any of them, they concluded that my children would partake of the usual complexion of the race, and they were horribly disgusted to find that this one had a strong tendency to whiteness. Many were the uncomplimentary epithets which were applied to the baby in Lamlam's hearing, on the occasion of the confabulation; for these people, in spite of their pretence to refinement (and they have as much of this as even European dames), were really, in most cases, heartless and cruel, not sparing the feelings of others—because they themselves had none. I had suggested a name to Lamlam, and expressed a wish that he might be called by the name of Philip. Such an uncouth, savage name could not, however, be heard of; so they gave him the name of Wŏkamshé. The ceremony of naming reminded me of another ceremony—that of baptism, and I felt that the child ought to be made a Christian, so I talked to Lamlam about it. The following conversation ensued:—

I explained first what baptism was. The pouring of water on the face—Lamlam called this "watering the baby."

"But what is the good of watering the baby unless his face is unclean?"

"It will make him a Christian, Lamlam, like Jesus Christ, of whom we read in the book; like the man who went on a journey in the 'Pilgrim's Progress'—that man was a Christian."

"But would Wŏkamshé go on a journey away from me if you watered him?"

"No, certainly not; but he would be a Christian, and would grow up kind and good. All white people are baptized."

"What! even those who kill one another with thunder and fire?" I had described battle-scenes to Lamlam.

"Yes, all of them."

"But then they are not good if they kill one another?"

I felt that my flank was turned by this remark, and I did not for a moment understand how I was to escape from the dilemma in which it placed me.

"If it does not make them good of what use is it to water their faces? Would it be better to put water on the whole body?"

I replied, remembering one of the answers in the Catechism, that to baptize him would make him "a member of Christ, a child of God, and an inheritor of the kingdom of heaven." Lamlam could not understand, nor indeed could I, but I tried to explain.

"A member of Christ! what is that?"

"A member is a part, a limb; this is a member," holding out my arm.

"How can this baby become an arm of Jesus Christ? Where is He? And how can he grow on to Him?"

Here again I was puzzled, so I put off my little wife by saying, "You see, Lamlam, I am ignorant myself, but I will talk to the book, and find out what it says. In the meantime we will call our little baby Philip, for the other name is exceedingly ugly."

I began to read the Bible, to learn what I could about baptism. So I read first the words, "Go ye out into all the world, and preach the Gospel;" "He that believeth and is baptized shall be saved." Philip was not old enough to believe, so this did not seem to apply to him. I then found the words of Peter, "Repent, and be baptized every one of you, for the remission of sins." For a similar reason the words could not apply to him. While I was thus examining various passages, by the help of the references in the Bible, I came across these words, "Your bodies are the members of Christ." These were the very words of the Catechism; so I read them eagerly, and turned up the other places to which the verse referred me. "Ye are the body of Christ;" "The Church which is His body," and here, I thought I could see my way. So, after the lapse of several days, for my studies took time, I said again to Lamlam,—

"To baptize Philip is to admit him into the Church; he will after he is baptized be a member of the Church.

"What is the Church; and whereabouts is it?" was her reply.

"Oh, the church is a place where Christians meet to worship God; where the minister preaches and prays."

"But how can you take him to the church? There is none in K'ootar."

This was true, and again I was perplexed. At last a happy thought struck me.

"You know, Lamlam, how my life was saved because I had been made a mason, and was able to give the sign to the old priest. Well, in the same way, if Philip is baptized he will become a Christian; and if ever he goes among the white men, he will be received as a Christian."

"Will you then put any mark on him; or how will they know that he is a Christian?"

"He will be able to tell them, and that will be enough. Everybody will be glad to see him, just as the Orangwŏks were glad to see me when I became an Orangwŏk."

I felt I was justified in exaggerating a little for the sake of the end to be obtained. So at last Philip was baptized. The birth of Philip had made me feel very serious, as I did not like the idea of his being brought up a heathen. After baptizing him I felt very much easier in my mind.

Little Philip did not thrive like European children; he remained weak and sickly, inheriting his mother's constitution as well as her gentle nature. But although he often occasioned us much uneasiness, yet he brought a large amount of happiness into the house, for he was treated like the child of civilized parents. He sat with us at table, prattled with us, and Lamlam was very fond of him. Indeed, I never saw a European mother more devotedly attached to her white chubby child, than was she to her little olive-coloured, sickly baby. So too was I. We never cared to let him out of our sight, and called to one another to observe all his little ways. If one was absent when he accomplished any feat of speech, or manner, or movement, all was duly related by the one who had witnessed the baby marvel. In this way our household was in striking contrast to the households of the other chiefs. Amongst them the children were never, or very rarely seen; they were kept by the slaves, so that the chief's house should not be disturbed, and the chief's wife should be free to attend to the amusements of her people. One of these amusements was a remarkable one. The chiefs and their wives (young women were not permitted to be present until they were married) met at a large room, especially built for the purpose, and on all being assembled (the women in a disgustingly nude state, having on only some gold ornaments) a chief, dressed in all the colours of the rainbow, with a long wand in one hand, entered the room, holding a number of light, downy-looking feathers in the other hand. These he distributed—one to each chief. When all was ready, the signal was given by the beating of drums and the playing of music; at which each chief and his wife started down or across the room, blowing this feather before them. It was wonderful to see the agility and cleverness that was displayed in keeping this piece of down in the air; and it was amusing to see the whole crowd at this game, men and women jumping, bobbing, blowing — endeavouring to keep the feather up. One by one, however, the crowd would retire as the feather each had been trying to keep alive fell to the ground, those who thus retired arranging themselves round the room, to watch the efforts of those who remained still on the floor. At last a solitary pair alone remained, and these were completely exhausted; they, however, kept up with wonderful spirits, jumping at times frantically, and puffing as if the last breath of life was passing from them. At last these too collapsed—utterly done up; and sometimes, I am told, the women were very ill from the exertions made on such occasions, for these amusements (if they can be called such) were kept up for hours. The thing seemed to me to be foolish enough itself; and when it is considered that it was very frequently dangerous, I was surprised that the good sense of the Orangwöks had not discouraged the silly game. After being at one of these "shun-shun," and witnessing the indecency of the costume, and violent exertion made by those taking part in it, I refused to attend any more, although by this refusal I believe I made several enemies who afterwards became very bitter towards me.

CHAPTER XXII.

And now it might be supposed my lot was cast in with the Orangwŏks, that I should never again see European civilization, and so it would have been, had not a serious calamity befallen me, by which I perforce escaped from captivity, and thus am able to give this narrative to the world. Our little boy was now two years old, but was not strong—far otherwise, he was exceedingly delicate, and I fear the European method of training, which I adopted with him, was not the most conducive to his health—at least such are my thoughts now. The reader has anticipated my story. The child who was so dear to us was taken very ill, and appeared to be sinking rapidly. Nothing could be done to save him, very little to relieve him, although everything that the most devoted and untiring affection could suggest and accomplish was done. Still the little sufferer sank gradually and steadily, until I had to confess that there was no further hope of his recovery to be entertained. As he was two years and a half old, and exceedingly intelligent, he understood much that was said and done.

"Papa, Philip's head is hot; put water on it, and make it cool."

"Yes, my dear, you will be better soon, please God."

"Will Jesus make Phil well, papa?"

"Yes, dear, He will. He will take you to heaven to be with Him for ever."

"But will you and mamma be there too. I don't want to go without you both."

"No, darling Philip," burst from the lips of his mother. "You shan't go without us. I will pray to Jesus to take us all together."

"There, there," said the little sufferer, "don't cry, Phil will be better soon," and he threw his arms round the neck of his mother, with great tenderness.

If Christianity brings its troubles, it certainly brings its joys. If it enlarges our capacities of suffering, it also enlarges our capacities of joy. Little Philip's tenderness, so unusual, so far beyond his age, greatly comforted both Lamlam and myself. I repeated the words, quietly, slowly, and clearly, "Suffer little children to come unto Me, for of such is the kingdom of heaven." They had a new meaning to me now. Philip was going softly, sweetly to the wonderful speaker.

"Yes, papa," he said gently, "I am coming. 'Of such is the kingdom of heaven.'"

He had learned the words weeks and weeks before. As the words passed from his lips, Philip was in the bosom of Jesus. Only his little warm body remained with us, lying upon his soft bed.

I need not speak of my wife's grief, nor of my own. Our love for our child was much greater than that felt by the Orangwöks usually, for he had been treated as a part of ourselves, and had in all things held the foremost place in our thoughts.

I was resolved that his body should not be burned, according to the custom of the country; that it should have Christian burial, and in the end I obtained my way. A little grave was dug in our park, and early in the morning his body, in a small box made under my directions, was carried to the grave, and lowered into the hole, as I read the funeral service over his mortal remains.

Never did I feel how beautiful and consoling was this service until now. It assured me of a resurrection to eternal life at His appearing, for I knew that my Philip slept in Jesus.

Lamlam and myself now redoubled our interest in the study of the Bible. I longed to obtain all the comfort it contained for myself. I was equally desirous of communicating it to my wife.

"You said, Trégan, that our Philip will live again in heaven beyond the sun. How can he get up there? He is in the earth. Will God send an angel to carry him up, and if so, how long will it be before he is taken away?"

"You do not quite understand, Lamlam. Philip's soul has gone to heaven—that which loved his papa and mamma—that which spoke to us through his soft eyes, and gentle hands—*that* was Philip, and that has gone to dwell in heaven with Jesus."

"But will not his body be in heaven too, his beautiful eyes, his nice winning ways. Will not these be in heaven?"

"Yes, Lamlam, yes. On the day of the resurrection. Let me read to you how Jesus rose from the dead, and then the chapter contained in the burial service."

I read and explained these, as she listened to me intently, the tears rolling down her cheeks.

A few days after this conversation, I picked up a chrysalis, and knowing something of the wonderful change through which it passed in becoming a butterfly, I put it away, carefully drawing Lamlam's attention to it. It looked like a dead body, she said. After the lapse of some weeks, I noticed that the change was at hand, and directed Lamlam again to consider it most attentively. Carefully stopping up every means of egress in the room, I waited the result. Next morning, taking my wife into the room, I approached the spot where the grub had been left. The shell or crust was there, but nothing else.

"Alas! it is nothing," she cried. "Will dear little Philip be like this?"

"No, Lamlam, like this," I said, drawing her attention to a beautiful butterfly that was now fluttering about the room.

With a cry of surprise and joy, she grasped my arm, and said,—

"Did that come out of this ugly piece of skin?" pointing to the outer covering.

"Yes, and in the same way, in the resurrection, our little Philip shall arise, a beautiful body, out of that weak, suffering body which was laid in the grave. 'Sown in corruption, raised in incorruption; sown in weakness, raised in power.'"

Her mind could now better understand the idea of the resurrection, and she derived great comfort from this illustration. At this time she proposed that we should ask others to join us in reading our Bible. To this I consented, and accordingly Kayhar, Lanna, the old priest Wannoota, with the wives of the former two, were asked to join us. They came very gladly, especially Kayhar and Lanna. The latter was a very thoughtful and religious kind of man, and had reflected much on our previous conversation. After reading a portion of the Gospel of St. Matthew, I translated it, as well as I could, into Orangwök. I found my auditors deeply interested, especially with the account of the crucifixion—most of them were in tears at this. It had never occurred to me to read this before. Again and again I was asked to read it, and on every occasion I found a similar result. I could not here help the feeling, that our familiarity with these Bible stories probably robs them of their great charm. At any rate, I can testify that the Orangwŏks were penetrated with lively emotions of sorrow as I read, and that they seemed to become better people, after hearing what they did. I cannot say this of all of those who were present. The priest was not I think affected by what he heard, but he was interested. Many others came, until my room was sometimes full of listeners. Lanna suggested that as so many were interested in these readings, it would be a good plan to write them out, and teach the Orangwŏks to read them. I felt under some constraint to do this, for I now began to feel my responsibility as a Christian towards these poor heathens. My dear little wife helped me much, so too did Lanna, who was an apt scholar, and in one year great progress was made, in both teaching them to read, and in writing the stories of the Gospels on paper. It must not be supposed from this that a great deal was done. All that I mean is this; some ten or twelve people learned to read a few words, and were able to make out two or three stories, copied out of Christ's Parables. But as they did not all have the same stories, the whole that was being read amounted to a considerable quantity, as much as seven or eight chapters altogether. During this year I was happy, so too was Lamlam; although we never forgot our great loss, yet in doing what we could to teach others about God, we were consoled.

CHAPTER XXIII.

I CONTEMPLATED the results of our religious teaching with satisfaction, and felt that now I was doing something that justified me in calling myself a Christian. My thoughts frequently reverted to dear Miss Cunningham, and I wondered whether she, from her heavenly home, looked down upon me and Lamlam. If so, I knew she looked with approval, and rejoiced that her lessons had not been entirely thrown away upon me.

On my saying this to my wife, to whom the whole of my history was known, she asked,—

"Do you think she can see us here in Tannavorkoo?"

"Yes, Lamlam, I do. She can look down from heaven to any part of the world."

"And do you think she loves me, as well as you, Trégan?"

"Yes, indeed, for she was as gentle and kind as Lamlam herself."

"Then she will love dear little Philip, and will take care of him until we go up to him."

"Jesus will take care of him. He has said, 'Suffer little children to come unto Me.'"

"Yes, but Jesus cannot nurse all the babies Himself. See what a lot of babies die even in K'ootar. He will want nurses for them all, and He can give our Philip to your friend. I am sure, from what you have told me, that she will be very kind to Philip; and now I feel quite happy about him. Sometimes I have felt sad, thinking of him wandering through the vast heaven without a mother to look after him; and although Jesus and the angels are kind, yet they could not be to him as a mother. But your friend could, and she would be one to him, for she loved you."

Lamlam did not say all this at one breath. She took some time to say it, and this was the sense of all she said.

She had never been strong, even when I first knew her, eight years ago, and latterly, particularly since little Philip's death, she had become weaker. I regarded her at times with an anxious heart, and at last acknowledged to myself that she had some chest disease. In the winter a violent cold settled on her lungs, and she was not able to shake it off. It clung to her right through the winter, until she was confined entirely to her own room. For some time before this, however, at her request, I had—once a week at least—read some portion of the Service in the Prayer Book for public worship.

"You said, Trégan, that Christians in your country meet together to worship God. In what way do they worship Him?"

I explained, and read the Service to her. It was after this that she suggested that we should join in similar acts of worship, and invite her father and mother, with Lanna and his wife, to join us. All this was done, and I never before so thoroughly enjoyed the public prayers of our Church.

Lanna and Kayhar enjoyed them also, and even Lamlam's mother, a hard, cold woman, seemed stirred by these acts of worship.

Lamlam herself seemed wrapt in a devotional state of mind and heart. After several of these acts of worship had been held, she said to me,—

"I begin now, Trégan, to understand something about the happiness of heaven. It was all a mystery. Now I can feel what it is to speak to God in prayer with others. The presence of others speaking the same words helps me to pray more warmly. I am so thankful that God sent you here, Trégan. I never should have known Him if you had not come. I should have lived and died a heathen—should have had no little Philip, no Trégan to love, no Jesus to rejoice in, no heaven to hope for. I am so thankful that you came," she said, throwing her arms round me.

She gradually became weaker. There was no doubt in my mind that she was dying. I could not contemplate such a result with calmness. I redoubled all my attentions, and read to her assiduously; I even prayed for her in my own words. Yet the end came on, and came quickly at the last. After she was confined to her room, and latterly to her bed, her mother was constantly with her. Lamlam spoke to her, and told her all she had learned from the Gospels—said that she could now die in peace and happiness.

The conversations made a very serious impression on her mother, and I have reason to believe they led her to take greater interest in the stories and teaching of the Gospel. Poor old woman, she was really attached to her daughter in her own way, and was overwhelmed with grief at the prospect of her death. Lamlam's father was most tenderly attached to her, and was continually with her whenever his duties permitted.

At last the end came. She held her last conversation with me—too sacred to be written here, except a few words of it.

"Will your friend be glad to see me, Trégan, in heaven?"

"Yes, dear, very glad; so too will little Philip. But, above all, the Lord Jesus will be glad that you have gone to His beautiful house."

"Will it be long before you come, Trégan—many years, or will you come soon?"

"That is as God wills, Lamlam. I am willing to go now if He wishes it."

"Come to me soon. I will talk to Philip about you, so that he shall not forget you, for he will soon be big, you know. We will keep a place by our side, and wait for you. When you come, will you love your friend, or Philip and Lamlam most?"

"You and little Philip, dear, be sure of that."

"Farewell to Trégan. 'Come unto Me, all that travail, and are heavy laden; I will give you rest.' 'In My Father's house are many mansions.' 'I am the way,'" and in murmuring these words, dear Lamlam passed from earth to heaven. She was dead.

P

I never knew till that moment how much sorrow the human heart could bear. I did not think I could have loved any human being so tenderly, so completely, and I was utterly prostrated by the blow. So too was her father.

We laid her in the same grave as dear little Philip. The one grave contained all that had been dear to me, and all that had brightened my life in K'ootar. Now I did not care to remain any longer, except that I was unwilling to leave the dust of those who were so dear to me. I put up a cross over their heads, and engraved upon it their names, both in Orangwök and in English.

One of these days some English missionary may find this symbol of Christianity amid the Tannavorkoo mountains, and will then know that some Christian man has already been before him, and that some Christian souls have passed away in K'ootar.

CHAPTER XXIV.

LAMLAM had fallen a victim partly to her own natural weakness of constitution, partly to a serious epidemic which was attacking many of the Orangwŏks—a chest affection beginning in an attack of the bronchial tubes, ending in congestion of the lungs, which carried off numbers of persons. Such a visitation had never been experienced before. It awakened the gravest consideration, which led to some results of a serious nature to myself. A meeting of the ŭŏŏ was convened to deliberate upon the anger of Otaroo, who was hiding his face in a most unusual way. All that happened at this council I shall never know, except that some serious charge was then made against myself and the religion which I professed. Lanna afterwards told me that Wannoota attended —he was a member of the ŭŏŏ, and as priest of Otaroo declared that his blessing would be withheld—that the seed should not germinate, nor the flower bloom, nor the people rejoice in health until his rival was driven from K'ootar. The priest declared that another god than Otaroo was worshipped, that Otaroo was deprived of his dues, and that he had borne this with long-suffering for three years, trusting that his children would turn again to him. As they had not done so, but had continued in their apostasy from him, Otaroo had at last sent his plagues upon them. This sickness was the hand of Otaroo.

"Where is there another God?" exclaimed the gruff voice of a counsellor. "Who in K'ootar worships any other god than the great Otaroo?"

"There is one," replied the priest, "who is the priest of another god. One who came among us from the Kahshir in the form of a white man, but who is really only a Kahshir disguised. Trégan is that priest," said Wannoota, with boldness in his tones. "And Otaroo has smitten him by killing both wife and child."

A great sob came from one corner of the darkened council-chamber at the allusion to Lamlam and Philip. Thus much was told me by Lanna, who had gathered this from his father-in-law, who was one of the ŭöö

In vain did old Kayhar, and one or two of my friends, attempt to stay the torrent of superstitious feeling that had been aroused by the crafty old priest. And, after much deliberation, a course was decided upon with reference to myself, which was at once to be carried into effect. All had been in readiness, for Wannoota knew that I had many friends in the council. Of what was going on I had not even a suspicion. Overwhelmed with sorrow as I was by the loss of my dear wife, I took no note of the ominous talk of Otaroo's anger. On the afternoon of the council, I was busy arranging the grave which marked the spot where the bodies of my wife and child lay. I wished to make it look as much like a Christian grave as I could, and had planted numerous seeds, together with a seedling tree of the cypress kind. Here I was engaged, several slaves assisting me, when an officer of the troops approaching me, said he had a communication for me from the ŭŏŏ. I immediately invited him to my house. On entering, I found myself in the presence of half a dozen well-armed Orangwŏks. I was their prisoner. I was not told the reason or cause of my arrest. I was simply told that I was a prisoner, and that if I attempted to escape, my death would be the penalty. At once I was conveyed to the prison—a large safely-built place surrounded by guards. Here I was kept for several days, no friends being permitted to see me, or communicate with me. I did not care much for life—a little while before I should have hailed death as a deliverer. Still, I desired to live, and was anxious to ascertain what it was intended to do with me.

I could obtain no information from any one. The old priest visited me, professing to be my friend. He exhorted me to pray to my God for deliverance, but gave me no hint, either as to the crime with which I was charged, nor as to my intended fate. Indeed he professed to know nothing. The only comfort I was permitted to have was the luxury of a bath, which I took regularly. To my surprise, on the third day of my confinement, I found the colouring-matter with which I had been stained, coming off my skin. I was as white as of old. As I looked upon my skin returning to its natural colour, I thought, can all this about Tannavorkoo and K'ootar be a dream. Am I really among civilized people, having been only dreaming of the Orangwŏks and their customs? The face of the old priest dispelled any such fancy. For there he was, witness to my change of colour. He started when he saw me, and professed surprise.

"Otaroo is angry, Trégan; what have you done? He has withdrawn his favour from you. You are lost," and immediately went out.

I did not like the look on Wannoota's face. The same evening I was taken before the ŭŏŏ. I had frequently heard of this council, and knew that it was all-powerful,—that from its decision there was no appeal. So I did not go without trepidation. Yet I knew I had friends in that council, and this thought encouraged me. On entering a large bare room, I was blindfolded, and then, led by the hand of one of my guards, I felt that I was being taken down some steps. On reaching a kind of landing, another hand was laid upon me, and the thought flashed through my mind that they were going to assassinate me. As I had never heard of an instance of assassination in all my stay in K'ootar, I put the thought from me, and yet the recollection of the mysterious fate of Lakangéoo (the old priest) produced in me a vague fear which was exceedingly unpleasant. The hand of the first guard was withdrawn from me, and I heard footsteps ascending, as if he was returning. My new conductor led me down still farther, and again I was transferred to another guide or conductor. After several such changes had been made, without a word being spoken on the part of any one, I felt that I had reached a room where several persons were gathered together. Here my eyes were unbandaged, but I could see nothing. I wondered, have I been blinded? has my sight been destroyed? and exercised my eyes to discover what was the matter with me. I could discover nothing. On reflecting that my sight could not be destroyed without my being conscious of great pain, I came to the conclusion that I must be in a darkened chamber, and suspected that I was in the council-room of the ŭŏŏ. I now heard voices subdued, as if coming from a distance, but could hear nothing distinctly. As I thus stood in suspense, surrounded by a darkness that might almost be felt, hearing the gentle breathing of others around me, feeling exceedingly nervous, a sudden movement in front occurred and a slight wind brushed past me. A hand again took hold of me, and I was led on. A few more steps, and I felt myself in the presence of the ŭŏŏ. A hand touched mine in the dark, and pressing it assured me of the presence of a friend. At this I took heart, and stood silently waiting the end. No one who has not been in it, can realize the solemn, fearful nature of such a position. Palpable darkness, dead silence, as if one was in a vast solitude, broken only by the strange sounds which warned one that there were other spirits present besides oneself. At last this fearful silence was broken by the voice of one of the ŭŏŏ—that of the president or principal chief.

"Trégan, you are summoned before a council of Hotarwŏkoo ŭŏŏ, accused of bringing upon the kingdom of K'ootar the anger of Otaroo by the introduction of another God. You are permitted to reply to this charge."

All the danger of my position rushed into my mind as the chief spoke—the treachery of the priest, the epidemic that had visited the people, the death of my wife and child, the cruelty of heathenism. What could I reply? In a moment of enthusiasm and recklessness, I replied,—

"That I do not worship Otaroo is true. I have never concealed the fact. I have, as a white man, been taught to worship another God—the God who made heaven and earth, the sun, the moon and stars. I do not believe that Otaroo is angry in consequence of this. It is mere superstition to think so. Let those who know what I have read to them from my sacred book say whether my religion is not good. If it is, Otaroo cannot be angry with it."

I ceased, and the silence which followed could be felt.

"Is it not true that your sacred leaf says, 'Whoso sheddeth slave's blood, shall be hung in a tree by the gods to rot?'"

It was the voice of the priest who spoke, remembering the words I had quoted in order to save the life of the slave, on the occasion of my marriage.

I replied,—

"Yes, these words are in my sacred leaf, and they are true. My God does not allow man's blood to be shed. He is angry when it is done."

Again the voice of Wannoota,—

"Otaroo has commanded that slaves shall be sacrificed. It is his due. We are all his. Your God forbids such sacrifice. He is then contrary to Otaroo—which is the stronger?"

"The God which I serve is the greater, for He made Otaroo and all things."

Again the priest replied,—

THE TRIAL.   Page 219.

"Trégan was made an Orangwŏk, and became sun-coloured. Otaroo gave him a wife from the Orangwŏk chiefs. Otaroo gave him a son. All was well, but Trégan went in his heart back to his own God; then Otaroo took from him his son, to warn Trégan that he must return. But Trégan continued to seek for other gods, and invited many Orangwŏks to join him in his search. Again Otaroo turned away his face, and Lamlam, the daughter of a chieftain, of an ŭŏŏ died. Otaroo continues angry, and K'ootar will not see his face until this enemy is destroyed. Otaroo gave Trégan the colour of the sun. He has now taken it away. Trégan is no longer an Orangwŏk. His skin is white like his heart."

After a moment's silence he continued,—

"Judge, O wise men, of the anger of Otaroo when he has restored Trégan to his original colour."

At this instant a bright flash of light lit up the vast room, and the long robe in which I had been enveloped—head, face, and body—fell from me to the ground. I stood before the assembly of chiefs white as I was originally. The darkness returned again in a moment, and the priest repeated,—

"Judge, O counsellors of Hotarwŏkoo;

judge, O worshippers of Otaroo. See the evidence of his anger. Judge wisely."

The flash of light had revealed a room filled with dusky counsellors. Among them were Kayhar and Lanna's father-in-law. These were the only two that I could be assured were my friends. I could say nothing further. I could not explain how I had become white. I did not even suspect at that moment that the change was occasioned by the water of my bath, which had been prepared to bring about this result. I am sure now that such was the fact. I did not even suspect it while I stood before the council.

The fact of my having been restored to my original colour made a great effect upon the ŭŏŏ; nothing could resist the force of this evidence.

After I had been reconducted to my prison, the ŭŏŏ proceeded to deliberate upon the punishment I should receive. The priest Wannoota insisted that I should be put to death, to pacify the wrath of Otaroo; and his arguments for a while prevailed. But Kayhar and Lanna's father-in-law resisted this determination, and were ably supported by the old warrior who had fought with me against the Tokshis. To me, he said, the king owed the preservation of Wätárá. As I was well known, there was an evident unwillingness to put me to death. Yet such would have been my fate, probably, had not my friends resorted to a stratagem. Kayhar said, that if I was a priest of another god it would not be wise to provoke this god to anger by killing me, that although Otaroo was great, yet, that as powerful kings were sometimes overcome by weaker ones through adverse circumstances, so the God of Trégan might, by some chance, prove himself a match for Otaroo. Kayhar would therefore advise that I should be restored to my own God beyond the sea, and so the kingdom be ridden of any further danger from the introduction of new gods.

In this defence Kayhar dissembled his real feelings and opinions, and gave the advice which I have related from a desire to save my life, which he saw was in imminent danger of being sacrificed. This speech of his produced a profound impression, and at last a conclusion, recommending the king to expel me from his kingdom, was agreed to, Wannoota having to be content with this.

CHAPTER XXV.

The first intimation I received of the decision of the ŭŏŏ was from Kayhar the same evening. He came to me in my prison, bringing authority for my release, as he had made himself responsible for my safe keeping.

"Your life is safe, Trégan, but you must leave the kingdom of K'ootar. This was the only leniency that your friends could procure for you."

And then he proceeded to tell me all that I have narrated, in the previous chapter, of the deliberation of the ŭŏŏ.

"I am thankful we were able to protect your life. I regret that we could not keep you with us. We shall, however, never forget you, nor shall we forget all that we have read in the 'white leaf.' We shall keep those stories and learn them by heart, remembering that Trégan brought them to us."

By this time we had reached Kayhar's house, and on my entering I was overcome by my recollections of the past, for I saw, as if it was only yesterday, little Lamlam coming again to learn from me ; to take her farewell when I started for Wătárá. I saw again all her gentle, winning ways, and was thoroughly cast down. I should never see her again, nor should I again look upon these scenes of her past life. In a few hours they would be gone for ever. Such thoughts tended to make me very sad, and I fear I was not much of a companion for Kayhar. Later in the evening Lanna came in to see me and to welcome me on my escape from the toils of the old priest Wannoota. He had, through Kayhar's influence, been appointed to escort me to the boundary of the kingdom. Of this I was exceedingly glad. We were to start at sunrise next morning, as it was considered desirable by my friends to get me away before any change could be brought about in the minds of the members of the ŭŏŏ. I retired that night, but not to sleep, for I was too excited to repose myself. I made every preparation for my departure before lying down. I had only one purpose to fulfil before leaving K'ootar for ever. Before the sun rose I was at my post to execute my purpose; to make a sketch of dear Lamlam's and Philip's grave. I knew the sketch would be very rough and hurried, but it would serve as a memento of that which was dear to me. As I sketched the silent heap, with its small white cross, looking so still and solemn in the early light, I saw the rays of the sun tinting the snow-topped peaks of Tannavorkoo, As I watched, fascinated by its golden glories—for I had not seen the sun for some weeks—I endeavoured to express what I saw on my sketch. The light stole downward rapidly, and, sweeping along the plains, touched the tree-tops in my park, and flooding them from branch to root, lighted up the little grave and its white cross. It was the light of another morning brightening upon me. I wish to keep those sensations for ever. I was aroused from my reverie by the voice of a slave, telling me that Lanna was waiting for me. After a long, painful, and eternal farewell with Kayhar and his wife, the parents of Lamlam, I passed from K'ootar for ever. For a time we were all silent; every mind was filled with sorrowful reflections, but after the first few miles were past, and the cool fresh air had invigorated us, we began to talk.

"Your coming has been good for us, Trégan," said Lanna; "I am sorrowful at your departure."

"Just think, Lanna, that I was killed in battle, and you will be able to think more complacently about my going away. I shall be just as if I was dead to you."

"If you had been killed in battle I should not have cared so much, but you have been betrayed by Wannoota, who hates you, and many of the chiefs have joined in his act because they are envious of you. They want to get rid of you. They do not believe old Wannoota's fable about Otaroo any more than I do. It suits them to accept the priest's view of these things."

"I am glad that they do not believe in Otaroo, they may thus come to accept a better religion."

"I do not mean that they do not believe in Otaroo. I mean that they have no fear of his anger. They know that all things would go on in very much the same way as at present, whether we worship him or not. However, I shall never worship him again, Trégan. I shall always worship Jesus, for after Lamlam's death I saw what belief in Him could do. It is my firm intention to adhere to Him as my God, and to learn His words."

We had now reached the descent to the first plateau. Before descending into it, we caught a glimpse of the lower plain, and saw the waters of the lake (Lake Ambá) lying far away on our left.

The scene was like a fairy scene—soft and graceful in the spring light. On our right lay the plateau, with its large town and numerous homesteads, well watered, and showing already signs of rich vegetation. But I need not repeat—I need not linger. I could not fail to recall the impressions made upon me nine years ago, as I was carried upward to the mysteries of the mountain kingdom. I wondered too, if I should ever return again to civilization and to France. I resolved to spare no efforts to escape to Australia, and I planned at this time a device, which I afterwards carried out, to get away from the Rahshĕs, or coast tribe. On the second day the boundary rampart was reached. We stayed at the first posting-house for the night. In the morning Lanna would go homeward; I would go eastward, towards the coast. At sunrise he and myself rode along the path by ourselves, to have a last quiet talk. After exchanging mementoes with each other, we parted in great sorrow.

Once on the natural rampart, I paused to look back over the kingdom of Tannavorkoo. It was a lovely sight that my eyes rested on. The mountain all glowing in the light, the lake glittering like a mirror, the smoke rising up gracefully beyond the tree-tops, the tall trees of many kinds, the bright-coloured flowers and birds. I could have returned, had not that little grave, which rose before my mind's eye, contained all that I loved.

I turned my course slowly to the coast— Lanna had given me the route, and I, as a sailor, knew something of the points of the compass. So I steered my course towards the scene of my first adventure in New Guinea. Without much difficulty, I could avoid the wandering tribes, through the speed of my little pony. I reached Ragek, on the second day towards evening. I rode up to the village, passing the old palisade in which I and my unfortunate companions had been confined. I passed the place of the great fire, marked by the presence of the vast slabs of stone, and shuddered to think of their fate. I was known and recognized instantly. All the village came to see and welcome me. I was installed at once in a place of honour.

CHAPTER XXVI.

I RESOLVED to carry out my scheme without loss of time. I knew something of the coast of New Guinea and Australia, and that some settlements were to be found along the northern parts of the latter. I knew too that it was quite a possible thing to reach the mainland in a small boat, although I shrank from attempting the voyage in one of the native canoes. Better make the attempt in a canoe, than remain for ever amongst savages. Such were my thoughts, and such my resolution. My scheme to escape from the hands of the Rahshēs was this: to pretend that I had the authority of Lakangéoo to go over to the mainland. I was at once questioned about the old priest, for he had never returned to them. To all questions I gave evasive, mysterious answers. I was acting under the directions of the priest of Otaroo, and was to take a canoe to the land beyond the sea. There was some resistance to this proposal at first, but my influence succeeded, and I went next day to the shore of the bay, mentioned at an earlier stage of this narrative. To my great delight I found the boat of the *Ville du Havre*. It had been picked up upon the coast by the natives, and repaired by them. As it had a sail and oars I resolved to use the boat for my attempt to escape to the mainland. A stock of provisions—yams, fish, meat, and fowls—was laid in, enough for a week or more. A large calabash of water, with a small quantity of Éw beverage, sufficed for liquids; and, feverishly anxious as I was to get away, when all was on board I felt inclined to cast off that night. However, I waited till Otaroo came up out of the sea, and then, without loss of time, cast off and sailed down the bay, accompanied by many canoes. I do not care to weary the reader with accounts of my voyage. Let it suffice to say that before dark I was well down the coast. On the second day I had rounded "South-East Cape," and had trimmed my sail for the Australian shore. The next day there was no land in sight, and the little boat danced like a cockle-shell on the heaving water. It made me feel very solemn to look up and around, and to see nothing but water and sky, and to know that I was thus alone with God. On the fourth day, towards sundown, I sighted a white sail, like the wing of a gull in the distance. As she drew nearer I saw that she was barque-rigged, and that she was crossing my course. I crowded on all sail, and felt my heart beating wildly. After ten years of captivity I shall see again the old world and home. But the thought of poor Philip lying in a watery grave dashed my joy a little. The ship kept on her way steadily. She had seen me—at least I thought so. She was putting her helm down. It was all right, I should be saved. Never shall I forget the pleasure of that moment. But the sun went down while she was yet a considerable distance from me. Soon it was quite dark. I could see, however, the ship's lights; could fancy—was it fancy?—that I could hear the water rippling by the ship's side. But she did not get nearer, and the darkness deepened. I shouted, but no answer came back; not even the echo of my own voice.

Hours passed, and I was still alone on the sea, unrescued, although so near to safety and home. During all the night, I kept a keen look-out, and watched with deepest anxiety. At times I saw the ship's lights, and thought she was lying-to until morning; at others I missed her altogether, and then felt that I had been given up. I plied the oars untiringly to keep up with the ship, and hoped that by dawn she would at least be in sight. When morning dawned, I was doomed to bitter disappointment. No ship could be seen. The horizon was perfectly clear. I watched the sun rise out of the ocean like a disc of fire, and saw his rays burnishing the world's great highway; but no ship, no indication of sail or spar could be seen by the increasing light. I was bitterly disappointed, and was undecided how to act. It was evident that there was a prospect of ships passing upward, that I might be picked up if I kept on my way. Should I pursue my way, or strike for the Australian shore? I decided to make for the coast, and to land upon the Australian continent. So, with rising hope, I turned my boat's head in the direction of the coast, guiding myself by the sun, Towards nightfall I sighted a dim bank, which my sailor's experience told me was land. So I determined to lie-to all night, lest if I attempted to approach the shore in the dark, I should be exposed to some danger. This I accordingly did, and, when the day broke, kept on my course towards land. Before noon I approached the shore, a rocky, bold outline and heard the heavy roll of ocean reverberating along the coast, and saw the spray spurting up over the cliffs. I coasted the shore for an hour before finding a place which permitted me to land. At last an opening presented itself, and into this opening I ran my boat, and then found that I was in still water, and able to run myself ashore. Thank God, I was at last on a civilized continent, It was a matter of time only to enable me to reach Moreton Bay. I formed no plans at once, but determined to rest myself, and wait until next day before doing so. In the night I slept in my boat, and slept soundly. But when morning came I was in the hands of a number of Australian savages. They had seen my boat coming towards the land, and had hidden themselves. During the night, or rather at the dawn of day, they had stolen upon me, and I was in their hands. They treated me kindly, and seemed very much interested in my fate. They, however, took everything I had, and destroyed my boat. No hope of escaping by that remained to me. A hopeless captivity must follow, unless some unexpected chance in my favour arose. From one captivity to another! Alas, I was utterly cast down. However, it is not my intention to relate in this place the particulars of my residence among the aborigines of the Australian continent. I lived among them for two years, and obtained much interesting information respecting their habits and beliefs. They behaved to me with unexpected kindness, which I can never repay. I found them capable of warm, generous impulses, and intelligent in a high degree. Their character is, I think, very much misunderstood by Europeans generally

CHAPTER XXVII.

Two years passed away—years which had been spent in the wildest portion of the great island. At one time in hunting; at another time in forays against some other tribe. I had thus learned that the interior of the continent was not a great desert, but was fertile and well wooded. There were, however, few mountains, and, consequently, few rivers of any size. The country was not at all like the interior of New Guinea. I always endeavoured to keep near the coast, in hopes of seeing a ship and obtaining deliverance through her means. And so it happened when the tribe was camped near a rocky headland, which ran out into the sea, that one evening before dark I had seen from the top of a hill, a white sail. I knew that it was the sail of a ship, and hoped that she was approaching the coast. I determined to make an effort to arrest their attention. When night came on I made a large fire in a conspicuous position, and kept it burning for some hours under the plea of driving away evil spirits. I saw the fire leap up higher and higher, and felt that such a glare would attract attention afar off, and warn those who saw it that there might be shipwrecked mariners thereabouts. Nor was I disappointed. My signal was seen. Towards morning I ran to the top of the cliff, and looked out across the ocean. I was overjoyed to see the ship standing off and on, while a small boat was pulling towards the headland. Running down to the shore, to the place which the boat was approaching, I was ready to welcome my deliverers. There were five in the boat, and on seeing me, the one at the helm, a sea-captain, hailed me,—

"Hollo, there! who are you, mate?"

"A shipwrecked sailor, captain, among the blacks."

"Any blacks about?" he asked, as he sprang ashore.

I explained, and he resolved to proceed with caution.

I need not prolong my narrative. My friends, the blacks, were unwilling to part with me, yet allowed me to leave them with many expressions of regret, and I was shortly afterwards taken on board the *Newcastle* ship. I was eagerly questioned on reaching her about my captivity and adventures, and endeavoured to satisfy the curiosity of my rescuers. After I had taken some refreshment, I was called aft to be questioned by the captain.

"What countryman are you?" he inquired, for I had several times spoken in Orangwŏk, and had indeed but an imperfect apprehension of English. I had not spoken it for twelve years.

"What countryman are you?"

"French, sir," was my reply.

"French!" he exclaimed, speaking in that tongue. "From what part of France do you come?"

"From the province of Maine."

"And what is your name, my man?" he asked, with great interest in his tones; "I too am from Maine, from the village of—"

"What!" I exclaimed, "you are not Philip Rigaud of the *Ville du Havre*?" I scanned his face closely, as I asked the question, but twelve years alter most men much and alter some men greatly; yet I could see, I fancied, a resemblance to my old friend. In another moment I threw myself upon his neck, and embraced him. I knew it was Philip who stood before me.

"You, Louis, you alive?" was all that he could say, in broken tones.

Philip was not dead. The wave had swept the boat away, had endangered the safety of the crew, yet had not swallowed them up. They had kept away from the coast, as the waves were breaking for miles along the shore. After the subsiding of the storm, they continued their course down the coast and endeavoured to reach the Australian continent. On the third day, a schooner, driven out of her course by the hurricane, picked them up, and they were saved.

* * * * *

Philip was now, and had been for several years, master of the *Newcastle* ship. He was able to offer me the post of second mate with him, which I gladly accepted. I am to be first mate shortly, and with this expectation I am content. I am with my old friend—the friend of my boyhood.

* * * * *

Once Philip had returned to France to his early home. His parents were dead. So too was my mother. She had, however, received my last letter before I sailed for New Guinea, and had been greatly comforted by it. "Alas! my mother, never shall I see thee again in this earthly life!"

My story is ended. The reader will, I trust, pardon all its faults.

THE END.

GILBERT & RIVINGTON, LTD., ST. JOHN'S HOUSE, CLERKENWELL RD., LONDON.

Uniform with this Volume.

With numerous Illustrations, 2s. 6d.; gilt edges, 3s. 6d. each.

Dick Cheveley. By W. H. G. Kingston.
Heir of Kilfinnan. By W. H. G. Kingston.
Off to the Wilds. By G. Manville Fenn.
The Two Supercargoes. By W. H. G. Kingston.
The Silver Cañon. By G. Manville Fenn.
Under the Meteor Flag. By Harry Collingwood.
Jack Archer: a Tale of the Crimea. By G. A. Henty.
The Mutiny on board the Ship "Leander." By B. Heldmann.
With Axe and Rifle; or, The Western Pioneers. By W. H. G. Kingston.
Red Cloud, the Solitary Sioux: a Tale of the Great Prairie. By Colonel Sir William Butler, K.C.B.
The Voyage of the Aurora. By Harry Collingwood.
Charmouth Grange: a Tale of the 17th Century. By J. Percy Groves.
Snowshoes and Canoes. By W. H. G. Kingston.
The Son of the Constable of France. By Louis Rousselet.
Captain Mugford; or, Our Salt and Fresh Water Tutors. Edited by W. H. G. Kingston.
The Cornet of Horse; a Tale of Marlborough's Wars. By G. A. Henty.
The Adventures of Captain Mago. By Leon Cahun.
Noble Words and Noble Deeds.
The King of the Tigers. By Rousselet.
Hans Brinker; or, The Silver Skates. By Mrs. Dodge.
The Drummer-Boy; a Story of the time of Washington. By Rousselet.
Adventures in New Guinea; The Narrative of Louis Tréganca.
The Crusoes of Guiana. By Boussenard.
The Gold-Seekers. A Sequel to the above. By Boussenard.
Winning his Spurs: a Tale of the Crusade. By G. A. Henty.
The Blue Banner. By Leon Cahun.
Ben Burton; or, Born and Bred at Sea. By W. H. G. Kingston.
Adventures on the Great Hunting Grounds of the World. By V. Meunier.
The Three Deserters; or, Ran Away from the Dutch. By M. T. H. Perelaer.
My Kalulu, Prince, King, and Slave. By H. M. Stanley.

Adventures of a Young Naturalist. By Lucien Biart. Edited and adapted by Parker Gillmore (Ubique).
The Startling Exploits of the Doctor. By Céllere.
The Brothers Rantzau: a Story of the Vosges. By Erckmann-Chatrian.
The Serpent Charmer. By Louis Rousselet.
Stories of the Gorilla Country. By Paul Du Chaillu.
The Conquest of the Moon. By A. Laurie.
The Maid of the Ship "Golden Age." By H. E. Maclean.
The Frozen Pirate. By W. Clark Russell.
The Marvellous Country. By S. W. Cozzens.
The Mountain Kingdom. By D. Lawson Johnstone.
A Thousand Miles in the "Rob Roy" Canoe. By John MacGregor ("Rob Roy").
Blacks and Bushrangers; or, Adventures in Queensland. By E. B. Kennedy.
Sir Ludar: a Tale of Love, War, and Adventure in the days of the great Queen Bess. By Talbot Baines Reed.
Wild Life under the Equator. By Paul Du Chaillu.
My Rambles in the New World. By Lucien Biart.
New York to Brest in Seven Hours. By A. Laurie.
Rob Roy on the Baltic. By John MacGregor, M.A.
Bevis. By Richard Jefferies. Edited by G. A. Henty.
The Cobbler of Cornikeranium. By Rev. A. N. Malan.
Strange Stories of Adventure. By Captain Mayne Reid.
The Aztec Treasure-House. By T. A. Janvier.
How Martin Drake found his Father. By G. Norway.
Roger Ingleton, Minor. By T. B. Reed.
Axel Ebersen, the Graduate of Upsala. By A. Laurie.
Sandy Carmichael. By C. J. Hyne.
The Priceless Orchid. By Percy Ainslie.
An Inca Queen. By J. Evelyn.
Voyage Alone in the Yawl "Rob Roy." By J. MacGregor.
Adrift in the Pacific. By Jules Verne.
The Purchase of the North Pole. By Jules Verne.

LONDON: SAMPSON LOW, MARSTON & COMPANY, LTD.,
ST. DUNSTAN'S HOUSE, FETTER LANE, FLEET STREET, E.C.

NEW ISSUE OF POPULAR BOOKS.

Small crown 8vo, cloth, 2s.; gilt edges, 2s. 6d. each.

Most of the following are especially adapted for GIRLS, for SCHOOL PRIZES, &c.

MISS ALCOTT.
1. Little Men.
5. Little Women, and Little Women Wedded.
11. Under the Lilacs. Illustrated.
12. Jimmy's Cruise in the "Pinafore."
14. An Old-fashioned Girl.
15. A Rose in Bloom.
16. Eight Cousins; or, The Aunt Hill. Illustrated.
17. Jack and Gill: a Village Story.
18. Lulu's Library. Illustrated.
19. Silver Pitchers.
20. Work, and Beginning Again: a Story of Experience. Illustrated.
27. Aunt Jo's Scrap Bag.
28. Shawl Straps.
29. Spinning Wheel Stories.

MRS. WHITNEY.
2. Hitherto: a Story of Yesterdays.
8. We Girls.
9. The Other Girls.
21. A Summer in Leslie Goldthwaite's Life.
22. Faith Gartney's Girlhood.
23. Real Folks.
39. The Gayworthys.

MRS. H. BEECHER STOWE.
25. My Wife and I.
24. Dred: a Tale of the Great Swamp.
30. We and Our Neighbours.
31. Ghost in the Mill, and other Stories.

E. P. ROE.
41. Nature's Serial Story.

CAPTAIN SAMUELS.
3. From Forecastle to Cabin. Illustrated.

W. L. ALDEN.
10. Adventures of Jimmy Brown. Illustrated.
38. Trying to find Europe.

PHIL ROBINSON.
4. In my Indian Garden.
13. Under the Punkah.

MADAME DE WITT.
26. An Only Sister.

C. DUDLEY WARNER.
32. In the Wilderness.
35. My Summer in a Garden.

X. B. SAINTINE.
33. Picciola: or, The Prison Flower.

SAXE HOLM.
34. Draxy Miller's Dowry.

J. SANDEAU.
36. Seagull Rock.

J. BUNYAN.
37. Pilgrim's Progress.

MRS. TOOLEY.
40. Life of Harriet Beecher Stowe.

LONDON:
SAMPSON LOW, MARSTON & COMPANY,
Limited,
ST. DUNSTAN'S HOUSE, FETTER LANE, E.C.